6/2

# THE TRUTH OF PAPAL CLAIMS

BY

RAPHAEL MERRY DEL VAL, D.D.

*Archbishop of Nicaea*
*Future Cardinal Secretary of State*

### A Reply to

## THE VALIDITY OF PAPAL CLAIMS
BY
F. NUTCOMBE OXENHAM, D.D.
*English Chaplain in Rome*

PRESERVING CHRISTIAN
PUBLICATIONS, INC.
Traditional Catholic Book Publisher
Boonville, New York
**2012**

*Imprimatur*
        HERBERT CARDINAL VAUGHAN
                      *Archbishop of Westminister*

English edition first published by
B. Herder in St. Louis Missouri with
Sands & Company in London, 1902

*Reprinted:* May, 2012
**Preserving Christian Publications**
ISBN: 978-0-9840139-0-6

All inquiries may be addressed to:

PRESERVING CHRISTIAN PUBLICATIONS, INC.
PO Box 211
Boonville, New York 13309
tel: (315) 942 6338
**www.pcpbooks.net**

# CONTENTS

|  | PAGE |
|---|---|
| PREFACE | ix |

Correspondence in the *Church Times*—The reason of this book ......... ix—xvi

INTRODUCTORY - - - - - - - - 1

Methods of argument—The point at issue.

## PART I

DOCTRINE OF THE SUPREMACY AND INFALLIBILITY - - 9

The Supremacy—The Proof from Scripture—S. Peter in relation to the other Apostles—Difference between individual Bishops and individual Apostles—The Catholic Episcopate—Infallibility—What it means and what it does not mean—The Proof from Scripture—De Maistre—The Bishops of Rome—The Founders and the Bishop—The Clementine Romance—The False Decretals - - - - - 9—32

## PART II

THE VENERABLE FATHERS - - - - - 33

Maldonatus and Bellarmine—S. Augustine's Retractations—S. John Chrysostom—S. Cyril of Alexandria 33—54

# CONTENTS

## PART III

**ARGUMENTS AGAINST THE SUPREMACY AND INFALLIBILITY**    54

"Ye shall be witnesses unto Me" (Acts I. 8)—The Election of S. Matthias—The Institution of Deacons—"They were sent" (Acts VIII.)—The conversion of Cornelius—The Council of Jerusalem—S. Paul rebukes S. Peter—The Epistles of S. Paul—The Epistles of S. Peter    54—80

## PART IV

**THE CONSTANT BELIEF OF EVERY AGE**    81

The Popes not silent in the Early Ages—S. Victor and the Eastern Churches—S. Stephen and S. Cyprian—The Text of S. Irenaeus    81—109

## PART V

**COUNCILS OF THE CHURCH**    110

Necessity and Utility—The Council of Nicaea—The Sardican Canon—The Second General Council—The Council of Chalcedon and the Twenty-eighth Canon    110—125

## CONCLUSION

**CATHOLIC ENGLAND**    126

The Venerable Bede—The Bishops of the Province of Canterbury—The "Branch Theory"—Newman and the Fathers    126—129

## APPENDIX

# INDEX

|  | PAGE |
|---|---|
| Introductory | 1 |
| The Supremacy | 9 |
| Infallibility | 17 |
| The Bishops of Rome | 23 |
| The Venerable Fathers | 33 |
| Maldonatus | 36 |
| Bellarmine | 41 |
| S. Augustine | 44 |
| S. John Chrysostom | 48 |
| S. Cyril of Alexandria | 52 |
| The Book of Acts | 54 |
| S. Paul | 76 |
| S. Peter's Epistles | 79 |
| The Constant Belief of Every Age | 81 |
| S. Victor | 93 |
| S. Cyprian | 95 |
| S. Irenaeus | 101 |
| Councils of the Church | 110 |
| The Council of Nicæa | 113 |
| The Sardican Canon | 114 |
| The Second General Council | 118 |
| The Council of Chalcedon | 120 |
| Conclusion | 126 |
| Appendix | |

# PREFACE

THE following correspondence appeared lately in the *Church Times*, and we publish it here, as explaining the reason of this little book:—

### ROMAN WAYS IN CONTROVERSY.

Sir,—May I ask your courtesy for the publication of the following letter, which I have had occasion to write to a Roman priest, whose main occupation here in Rome appears to be to entice straying Anglicans into the Roman fold:—

18, Piazza del Popolo,
11th March, 1902.

Rev. Sir,—I am informed that you are preaching a course of sermons in adverse criticism of a small book which I published on "Papal Claims." May I venture to express a hope that you will publish your criticisms in order that they may bear the test of examination, and, if necessary, of reply?

I have the honour to be,
Your obedient servant,
F. N. OXENHAM.

The Rev. Mons. Merry del Val.

P.S.—I reserve to myself the right of publishing this letter, together with any reply which you may think fit to make.

To this letter I have received no answer or acknowledgment.

I had reason, arguing from precedent, to suspect that Mons. Merry del Val would probably make statements in these sermons which he would not venture to publish; his silence goes far to confirm this suspicion.

It is not difficult to estimate the value of controversial statements which a preacher ventures to make to a select congregation, but which he does not venture to publish.

F. NUTCOMBE OXENHAM,<br>English Chaplain in Rome.

March 10th.


## ROMAN METHODS OF CONTROVERSY.

Sir,—May I venture to trespass upon your valuable space and say a word in reference to a letter of Dr. Oxenham's which appeared in your issue of the 14th of March. It is a fact that on the 4th of March (not the 11th) Dr. Oxenham addressed to me the letter which he has published and that I have not replied.

I should have been glad to do so, though unacquainted with Dr. Oxenham, had he not added the postscript which appears at the foot of that letter. Without commenting upon the form and tone of what he has written, I would have replied that I was willing to consider the utility of publishing my lectures, in accordance with his request, though it is questionable that such a course could substantially add anything to the arguments and facts expounded so ably in the following works to which I refer Dr. Oxenham:—"St. Peter: his Name and his Office," by T. W. Allies; "The Catholic Claims," by Richardson; "History of my Religious Opinions," by J. H. Newman; "The Primitive Church and the See of Rome," by Luke Rivington; and "England and the Holy See," by Spencer Jones, one of Dr. Oxenham's brother clergymen, not to

# PREFACE

mention other writers. I might have added that if Dr. Oxenham would take pains to refer to authentic sources and to the original works of the Fathers and of Catholic theologians he would find a good deal to change in such astounding statements as the following, which are contained in his little book:—1. That the "ultramontane Jesuit doctor (Maldonatus) acknowledges (what every patristic scholar knows) that all those great doctors of antiquity, and among them three of the greatest—Origen, Chrysostom, and Augustine—every one of them differs from modern Romanists, and gives other interpretations to this famous text (Matt. xvi.), which other interpretations do not give any countenance to Papal claims" (pp. 26-27). And on page 32 Dr. Oxenham sums up his conclusion thus: "We saw just now how the Jesuit Maldonatus *conclusively refutes* the Papal assertions as to the first text on which they rely." The italics are my own. Dr. Oxenham discreetly suppresses all that Maldonatus says of the testimony of those *very same* Fathers, and of many others, upon this text, and his explanation of how the various interpretations of this same text may be easily accepted and reconciled.

2. On page 33 Dr. Oxenham, quoting from Dr. Salmon, asserts that another Ultramontane Roman writer, Bellarmine, can quote nothing earlier than the eleventh century in support of the Catholic interpretation of the text in St. Luke xxii. 31-32, upon which Bellarmine hardly dwells, and he again discreetly suppresses Bellarmine's numerous quotations from the early Fathers upon the Primacy of St. Peter and upon his relative position to the other Apostles. These are but samples of Dr. Oxenham's methods of controversy and of the arguments which he uses to convince his guileless readers of the futility of Papal claims. They are

methods which I will leave others to qualify, as they deserve. Much as I may differ from the Anglican position and consider it untenable, I can willingly acknowledge that those who defend it with honesty and ability (and there are many) do not resort to such questionable methods of controversy as those which Dr. Oxenham has adopted in his little book.

It was not my intention before, nor is it my intention now, to be dragged into a controversy in the press with Dr. Oxenham. I therefore refrained from answering his letter, for I could not do so in any form without acknowledging the right, which he assumed, of publishing any reply which I might have thought fit to make.

R. MERRY DEL VAL,<br>Archbishop of Nicaea.

March 17th.

## ROMAN WAYS IN CONTROVERSY.

Sir,—I was unwilling to disturb the quiet of Holy Week by taking any notice of Mons. Merry del Val's letter in your issue of March 21st; but now I beg leave, by your kind permission, to make a few remarks on that letter.

(1) I admit readily that I did, in my book on "Papal Claims," make both the "astounding statements" to which Mons. Merry del Val objects; and hereby I distinctly reassert both those statements, because both of them are simply true, as Mons. Merry del Val might easily satisfy himself, if he would take the trouble to consult those "original works" to which he is kind enough to refer me. Your readers may do the like.

(2) I admit, with equal readiness, that I did (to use

# PREFACE    xiii

Monsignor's phrase) "discreetly suppress" those portions of the writings of Maldonatus and of Bellarmine to which he refers.

I should not myself use, in this sense, the word "suppress," but I quite agree that it is "discreet" to omit making long quotations which have no bearing upon the particular point in question.

This was the simple and, I think, sufficient reason for both those omissions of which Mons. Merry del Val complains.

Let me make this clear to your readers.

In the first instance, my purpose was to show that the assertions made by the Vatican Council and by the present Pope with reference to the famous passage in St. Matt. xvi. 18, were not true, those statements being that the Papal interpretation of this passage was "the venerable and constant belief of *every* age," and that it was held and taught by "*all* the venerable Fathers." (The italics are mine.)

For this purpose I quoted the Jesuit Maldonatus, who admits that three of the greatest of "the venerable Fathers"—Origen, Chrysostom, Augustine—every one of them differ from this Papal interpretation and adopt other interpretations, which do not give any countenance to Papal claims. The case of St. Augustine (shall I say that Mons. Merry del Val "discreetly suppresses" it?) is particularly strong, because, as I have shown in "Papal Claims" (pp. 27-28), St. Augustine in his younger days had interpreted "this rock" to mean St. Peter; but in a book which he wrote some years later ("Retractations," Book 1, cap. 21) he says he thinks the interpretation which he once gave, mistaken, and that "this rock" means Christ Himself. If the interpretation, which St. Augustine first gave, had been, as the Vatican Council declares that it was, the "constant belief of every age," it is inconceivable that St. Augustine should have thus quietly put it aside and adopted another interpretation.

Now if three of the greatest of "the venerable Fathers" did not hold or teach the Papal interpretation of this text, it is plainly false to assert that they "all" did so hold and teach.

That was my only point, and I repeat that what Maldonatus says as to Origen, Chrysostom, and Augustine, does "conclusively refute" the Papal assertions as to this text.

"All that Maldonatus says of the testimony of those very same Fathers and of many others," which Mons. Merry del Val accuses me of having "discreetly suppressed," is *nihil ad rem*.

No doubt Maldonatus quotes "many others" who agree with the Papal interpretation; and, of course, he thinks St. Augustine and the rest, who disagree, mistaken; and he tries to make out that they could not really have meant to differ from the Papal view. That is so, no doubt, and I make Mons. Merry del Val a present of that admission, if he cares to have it.

In the second instance of my "discreet suppressions" my point was to show that what Mons. Merry del Val is pleased to call "the Catholic interpretation" of the text in St. Luke xxii. 31-32, was not "the venerable and constant belief of every age." For this purpose I referred to the statement of "a recent learned writer" (Dr. Salmon, "The Infallibility of the Church," p. 344) who asserts that Bellarmine "can quote nothing earlier than the eleventh century" in support of this "Catholic interpretation" of this text. If nothing earlier than the eleventh century can be found in support of this so-called "Catholic interpretation," it is plainly false to assert that it was "the constant belief of *every* age." That was my only point; and it was proved. That Bellarmine makes "numerous quotations from the early Fathers upon the primacy of St. Peter, and upon his relative position to the other Apostles," is no doubt quite true. And it is equally true that I have "discreetly suppressed"—*i.e.*, not recited—any of those numerous quotations, because they were *nihil ad rem*.

These are the two instances which Mons. Merry del Val selects as illustrating my "questionable methods of controversy," and he gently intimates that there is some lack of "ability and honesty" therein. My method (at least so far as intention goes) has been to keep strictly to the exact point in question and to try to prove it, and not to endeavour to mislead unwary readers by going off on to side issues and trying to make capital out of them when you know that you have no case as to the main point at issue—*e.g.*, when you are discussing whether three particular writers did, or did not, make certain statements, and when you know perfectly well that they did make those statements, you should not attempt to divert attention by complaining that you have not been told what "many other" writers have said on the same, or a similar, subject.

The method which I have adopted appears to me to have the merit of "honesty," however much it may lack "ability"; whereas, in the other method, although there is great scope for "ability," there is not much room for "honesty." A suspicion that something of this latter method might have crept into the Monsignor's sermons in criticism of my little book was my reason for wishing that he would publish those sermons. I gather from his letter to you that probably these sermons will be "discreetly suppressed."

Here I take my leave of Monsignor Merry del Val, "Archbishop of Nicaea," of which venerable diocese he has about as much rightful claim to be the Archbishop as I have.

F. NUTCOMBE OXENHAM.

18, Piazza del Popolo, Rome,
    Easter Monday.

[We have allowed Mr. Oxenham his right of reply, but it is quite impossible to continue this controversy.—ED.].

The reader will find in these pages the substance of five lectures delivered in Rome at the beginning of this year. They formed part of a whole series on various subjects, and they were addressed to converts.

FEAST OF THE SEVEN DOLOURS, 1902.

# INTRODUCTORY

It is never a pleasing task to have to deal with an opponent who delights in sophistry, but when a writer forgets his good manners and finds it necessary to couch his specious reasoning in terms which are offensive and discourteous, the task becomes more displeasing still. Dr. Oxenham, in his little book entitled "The Validity of Papal Claims"—a book in which he endeavours to reply to the Pope's Encyclical on the *Unity of the Church*—appears to revel in abusive epithets, and he accuses Leo XIII. of "deliberate mistranslations and forgeries," of "most presumptuous" and "profane impostures," just as on a previous occasion he did not hesitate to charge the venerable Pontiff with having uttered a "deliberate and audacious falsehood."[1] But abuse is not argument, and I fancy that most people will be inclined to suspect that his position must be a weak one if it requires such weapons for its defence.

The main point at issue, as Dr. Oxenham himself acknowledges in the opening chapters of his book, is no other than this:—*Did S. Peter hold the privi-*

---

[1] See Dr. Oxenham's Letter to the *Guardian*, Nov. 23, 1896.

*leges of supremacy and infallibility now claimed for him, and were those privileges recognised by all the venerable Fathers of antiquity, and by all the holy and orthodox Doctors of the Church, as the Vatican Council asserts, and the present Pontiff teaches in his Encyclical on the Unity of the Church, according to the divine promise of our Lord and Saviour given to the Prince of His Apostles?*

1. Now, as regards Dr. Oxenham's manner of dealing with the subject, I must first point out that he seems to have experienced considerable difficulty when he came to translate the very simple text of the Vatican Council. No one in the least familiar with the terms of ecclesiastical language, or indeed with the etymology of words, would venture to translate "*discipulorum principi*" by "*the wisest of His Apostles.*" And yet, this is the version as it appears on page 8 of Dr. Oxenham's little book. However, after he had printed his book, Dr. Oxenham discovered his mistake, and in the copy which I possess,[1] there is inserted a strip of paper with some *Errata*, and we are asked to read *Prince* instead of *wisest*. It is not easy to pass over the mistranslation as a printer's error, and we are led to wonder how far we can trust Dr. Oxenham's manner of handling the texts which he quotes, and whether he is in any way competent to pronounce upon a

---

[1] A friend of mine has shown me a copy of Dr. Oxenham's book in which the correction does not appear.

translation given by Leo XIII., whom he accuses of "deliberately falsifying" the testimony of one of the Fathers.[1]

2. Dr. Oxenham proceeds at once to abandon the main point at issue, mentioned above, and, after the manner of the hero of Cervantes, to combat an imaginary foe. He adds page to page in order to prove that the Vatican Council and the Pope were wrong in saying that which they never did say. For nowhere has the Council or the Pope asserted that *all* the venerable Fathers and orthodox doctors of the Church, at *all times* and on *every* occasion, even when dealing with a subject other than the supremacy of S. Peter, have expressly described or expounded at length the position of S. Peter, or that each one of the Fathers has been at pains to mention that doctrine *every* time that he may have had occasion to refer to one or other of the three famous texts quoted by Dr. Oxenham, viz. :—" Thou art Peter, and upon this rock I will build My Church, and the gates of hell shall not prevail against it. And I will give to thee the keys of the kingdom of heaven. And whatsoever thou shalt bind on earth, it shall be bound also in Heaven; and whatsoever thou shalt loose on earth, it shall be loosed also in Heaven" (Matt. xvi. 18). "Simon, Simon, behold Satan has desired to have you that he may sift you

---

[1] Pages 82-85.

as wheat. But I have prayed for thee that thy faith fail not: and thou being once converted, confirm thy brethren" (Luke xxii. 31). "Feed my lambs. . . . Feed my sheep" (John xxi.).

We all know, and surely Dr. Oxenham cannot ignore the fact, that the Fathers often comment upon one same text in different ways, according to the particular doctrine with which they happen to be actually dealing, and that they frequently use the same text in support of several doctrines. Nor do they deny one of the doctrines because they are intent upon explaining another, and where there is no incompatibility between them. Now, I put it to the candid reader—Is it honest, is it fair, to quote the words of a Father in connection with one of the texts already mentioned, in a passage where that Father is not expressly discussing the supremacy of S. Peter, and perhaps only referring incidentally to this subject, and then, without allusion to all that the same Father has taught elsewhere, to conclude that he knew nothing of the supremacy of the great Apostle, and that the Pope is wrong in asserting that all the Fathers have acknowledged that doctrine? And yet this is Dr. Oxenham's method. Let me give an instance.

He discusses separately, I might almost say he dissects the three passages from Scripture above mentioned, and, with a flourish of trumpets, he professes to show that S. Chrysostom is not one of the "*venerable Fathers*" who taught the supremacy

# INTRODUCTORY 5

of S. Peter. He quotes a passage from one of that great doctor's homilies, in which, besides a number of other subjects, S. John Chrysostom comments upon the fall of S. Peter, and refers to the text: "Simon, Simon . . . I have prayed for thee"; and Dr. Oxenham concludes triumphantly with these words — "How entirely impossible would such a commentary as this be in the mouth of a modern Papalist! How entirely fatal to modern Papal claims in regard to this text is such a commentary in the writings of S. Chrysostom."[1] I intend dealing more fully, further on, with Dr. Oxenham's daring assertions in regard to the teaching of Chrysostom, and I shall show how Dr. Oxenham has suppressed the evidence connected with the point at issue, which is contained even in the very homily to which he refers us. But I would ask here—What right has he, in the name of sheer honesty, to present S. John Chrysostom to his readers in this way, in opposition to the Pope's assertion, without a word upon what that great doctor says upon the position of S. Peter? What right has he thus to leave his readers under the impression that S. John Chrysostom cannot be quoted as one of the venerable Fathers who taught the supremacy of S. Peter; which, as we have said, is the real point at issue? What would Dr. Oxenhan say if I were to argue that he admits Papal claims, by quoting some words of his at the

---

[1] Pages 34, 35.

end of his book without mentioning what is evident from all that he has written? By such a method, and with the help of sophistry of this kind, one might assert that Scripture denies the existence of God, and then turn upon a critic with the question—Does the Scripture say, or does it not say, that "There is no God"? Undoubtedly it does, but where? and when? and how?

3. Before a writer attempts to contradict a teaching, from whatever source it may proceed, it is essential that he should ascertain what that teaching really is, for otherwise he must inevitably employ his energies in beating the air. Now, Dr. Oxenham, when he comes to discuss the doctrine of S. Peter's infallibility, reveals the fact that he has not even understood the doctrine which he endeavours to overturn. On page 32, he comments upon the text of S. Luke xxii., and he writes as follows:—"Now, if these words of our Lord did indeed promise to S. Peter that he should be infallible and supreme, as we are told by the present Pope that He did, it is strange that shortly after this promise S. Peter should three times have actually denied his Lord— this did not look like infallibility." To say nothing of the fact that the Pope does not even mention that text on pp. 38, 39 of his Encyclical, as Dr. Oxenham declares that he does, his remarks suffice to show that Dr. Oxenham imagines, like so many other Protestants, that the Catholic doctrine of the infallibility of S. Peter and of his successors implies

# INTRODUCTORY 7

*impeccability*, which no Pope, no Council, no Catholic theologian ever dreamt of asserting. And Dr. Oxenham brings his mistake (should I say ignorance?) into further prominence when he speaks of the discussion between S. Peter and S. Paul, recorded in the epistle to the Galatians, and in regard to which, on page 58, he says—"For whether S. Peter's fault on this occasion were one 'of faith' or 'of fact,' whether his fault were 'light and venial' or not, the fact remains that he was in the wrong, that S. Paul withstood him before the Church, and openly rebuked him." If Dr. Oxenham had taken pains to find out what is really claimed for S. Peter and his successors by the Vatican Council and by the present Pope, and what Catholics mean by *infallibility*, he might have avoided stumbling into a blunder which does away with so many of his arguments.

4. Finally, we must place on record that Dr. Oxenham employs a method of controversy which he himself declares to be unfair. For on page 44 he writes as follows:—"It would not be fair to cite any of those passages in the life of S. Peter which are recorded in the Gospels, because it might be urged that our Lord did not confer on S. Peter his great privileges until the close of His own earthly ministry." Yes, exactly so, it would not be fair, or reasonable, as obviously S. Peter did not receive his office until the close of our Lord's earthly ministry, and therefore not until after the denial.

But this method of arguing which Dr. Oxenham pronounces not to be fair is precisely the one which he adopts all through the first half of his little book! He constantly refers to S. Peter's fall as an argument against his supremacy and infallibility, and he constantly recalls the comments of the Fathers upon S. Peter's sin as fatal to Papal claims. When an author thus adopts a line of argument which he himself declares not to be fair, there is little left for his critics to add.

# PAPAL CLAIMS

## PART I

A BRIEF STATEMENT OF THE DOCTRINE OF THE
SUPREMACY AND INFALLIBILITY OF S. PETER

### 1—*The Supremacy*

POPE LEO XIII.'s Encyclical on the *Unity of the Church* explains the Catholic doctrine of S. Peter's supremacy so clearly and so forcibly, that my readers have but to peruse it to convince themselves that Dr. Oxenham's assertions, to the effect that "the teaching of Scripture is plainly inconsistent with the truth of such a doctrine,"[1] and that the texts quoted by Catholics in support of that doctrine "each and all fail to declare, or even indeed, to allude to, any such doctrines,"[2] are undoubtedly bold assertions, but assertions that are contrary to fact. I will therefore only give a summary of the doctrine of S. Peter's supremacy and infallibility, but I will do so sufficiently to show, I trust, how little Dr. Oxenham understands the position which

---

[1] Page 16.   [2] Page 40.

he endeavours to contradict, and how futile are his arguments.

The two chief texts of Holy Scripture from which the Catholic teaching is drawn by the Vatican Council, by the present Pope, by the Fathers, and by our theologians, are the following:—1. "THOU ART KEPHAS (ROCK), AND UPON THIS KEPHAS (ROCK) I WILL BUILD MY CHURCH, AND THE GATES OF HELL SHALL NOT PREVAIL AGAINST IT. AND I WILL GIVE TO THEE THE KEYS OF THE KINGDOM OF HEAVEN. AND WHATSOEVER THOU SHALT BIND UPON EARTH, IT SHALL BE BOUND ALSO IN HEAVEN; AND WHATSOEVER THOU SHALT LOOSE ON EARTH, IT SHALL BE LOOSED ALSO IN HEAVEN" (MATT. XVI.). 2. "FEED MY LAMBS . . . FEED MY SHEEP" (JOHN XXI.). Three times our Lord gave this charge to Peter, and we cannot fail to note the progression, for He first speaks of the lambs, and then of the sheep in the most solemn manner. The text of S. Luke xxii., "SIMON, SIMON, BEHOLD SATAN HATH DESIRED TO HAVE YOU . . . BUT I HAVE PRAYED FOR THEE THAT THY FAITH FAIL NOT: AND THOU BEING ONCE CONVERTED, CONFIRM THY BRETHREN," significant as it is in the light of the two other texts, is often, though not always, quoted, and can be quoted in support of the same doctrines, but rather as cumulative evidence, together with other texts concerning S. Peter. Neither the Vatican Council nor the present Pope have said that this text of S. Luke, especially when taken separately from the other two, was *never* used by the Fathers to

## THE SUPREMACY

further emphasise some of Christ's teaching on other points of doctrine; and many "modern Romanists," as Dr. Oxenham would call them, very often hardly stop to dwell upon the text of S. Luke, after having proved S. Peter's position on the strength of what is said in the Gospels of S. Matthew and of S. John.[1]

Undoubtedly S. Luke's words are of great significance when taken in connection with the two most important texts already mentioned. I say in connection with those texts; for if we are to know what Scripture teaches us upon any subject we must consider all the texts that refer to that subject, and place them side by side, and in true harmony one with another. We shall thus be in a position to gauge their exact meaning and significance, since a teaching may not always be found fully expounded in one text. If we proceed, as Dr. Oxenham proceeds, to cut up the texts, there are many unquestionable and unquestioned doctrines of the Christian Faith which could not be proved by Holy Writ. When our Lord says, for instance: "I and the Father are one," if I follow the lines of Dr. Oxenham's argument against the supremacy of S. Peter, I might say that this text makes no reference to the Holy Ghost, and that the Fathers who have commented upon it, and spoken only of the Son, knew

---

[1] The Dogmatic Constitution of the Vatican Council rests chiefly, not to say entirely, upon the texts of S. Matthew and S. John, and only quotes the passage from S. Luke as further evidence on behalf of the same doctrine. (See Appendix.)

nothing of the existence of a third Person in the Blessed Trinity.

Now, with these texts before us, we hold, in union with the Vatican Council, that the Church, typified by Christ as an EDIFICE, as a KINGDOM, as a FOLD, rests upon S. Peter as a building rests upon its foundation, that it is ruled by S. Peter, to whom "the keys of the kingdom of heaven" were given, that it is led and provided with proper food by S. Peter, to whom the care of the whole flock was committed; a care which, our Lord says, was to be extended to the sheep as well as to the lambs, to the chief members of the flock, therefore, as well as to those who are dependent upon them. If the metaphors chosen by Christ Himself mean anything—and will Dr. Oxenham dare to assert that they mean little or nothing?—they must signify what we have just explained, and, accordingly, as we shall have occasion to point out, all the Fathers and Doctors of the Church have held this doctrine of S. Peter's supremacy, which, let us remember, is the matter at issue. We must not tire of recalling this in the face of Dr. Oxenham's evasions.

First, then, if Christ, the Divine Founder of the Church, the Corner-stone and Rock of the EDIFICE, the Divine Head and Ruler of the KINGDOM of heaven, the Divine Shepherd of the FLOCK, bestows separately and individually upon one of His disciples His own title, and calls him the ROCK of the EDIFICE here on earth; if He grants to that disciple

## THE SUPREMACY 13

the special powers of the RULER, by handing to him the Keys; if He, as the Divine Shepherd, on the eve of His Ascension, commits the care of His whole FLOCK to that particular disciple, with the powers of ruling ($\pi o\iota \mu a\acute{\iota}\nu\epsilon\iota\nu$) and of feeding ($\beta\acute{o}\sigma\kappa\epsilon\iota\nu$)—what, I ask, can be more evident than that Christ is here constituting an Office which is part of the very constitution of His Church, the necessary condition of Its stability, and of Its strength, and of Its unity? The Rock which is to sustain the edifice as the foundation upon which Christ builds must be essential to the whole construction. The Ruler who has the Keys must be indispensable to the whole kingdom. The Shepherd who is to govern and feed the whole flock of Christ cannot be absent from that flock, if it be really His. Does not all this imply universal jurisdiction, and a jurisdiction which Christ Himself has given, and which is therefore not an ecclesiastical development, but a Divine institution? Is "the teaching of Scripture plainly inconsistent with the truth of such a doctrine"? And do these texts "each and all fail to declare, or even to allude to, any such doctrine," as Dr. Oxenham asserts that they do?

Secondly. "What is needed is evidence to prove that S. Peter was on a wholly different footing from all the other Apostles, as the Pope, in the right of heritage, claims to be on a wholly different footing from all other Bishops." So writes Dr. Oxenham on page 24 of his book. Is not that evidence already clearly put before us in the texts above quoted? For on which of the Apostles did our Lord confer, in this most special way, the office and powers of the Rock, of the Ruler, of the Shepherd? To S. Peter alone and separately many things were given; whilst the other Apostles received nothing without him.[1] One alone can exercise the power which he received; their powers can be exercised by many. Their powers do not include his; but his powers include theirs. The Church was "built upon the foundation of the apostles and prophets, Jesus Christ being the chief corner-stone," to use S. Paul's words in his Epistle to the Ephesians.[2] But amongst the Apostles, one is chosen to whom special prerogatives are given. The Church is built upon the Apostles, but upon the Apostles *as Christ ranked them*, with their Prince at their head, who is endowed by Him with special prerogatives. Accordingly S. Paul speaks of the Apostles collectively, and he couples them with the Prophets, as authorised teachers of Divine truth. In doing so, S. Paul does not exclude but includes Peter, with whatever powers Christ gave him.

All the Apostles received a universal mission directly from Christ, nor had any one of them to apply to Peter for a mandate or for authority, though

---

[1] The power of binding and loosing was given to all the Apostles, including Peter, but to Peter alone and separately the power was especially given with the keys. See Appendix, Origen.

[2] ii. 20.

# THE SUPREMACY

their authority was bound up with, and dependent upon his own special supremacy. Dr. Oxenham is not aware of this, it would seem, or that this is the teaching of "modern Romanists"; and he is strangely led to argue off the point by quoting S. Paul's words to the elders of Ephesus: "Feed the Church of God which He hath purchased with His own blood,"[1] and the words of S. Peter, who exhorts his fellow-elders to "feed the flock of God,"[2] for the Pope to-day exhorts Bishops to feed the Church of God, namely, that portion of the Church which is committed to their care, but not independently of him nor of his own office over the whole flock. And, thirdly, there is a difference, a great difference, between individual Apostles and individual Bishops, though, as regards mission and authority, there is no difference between the Apostles, taken collectively, and the body of the Catholic Episcopate. The personal prerogatives of the Apostles, considered individually, ceased necessarily with their mortal career, because they were personal. But the prerogatives of the Apostolic Office in Peter could not cease with his life, because that Apostolic Office in *him* was not merely personal, but was established by Christ as an essential and necessarily enduring element in the very constitution of the Church. Hence that special Office must last as long as the Church herself remains, namely, to the end of time. The body of the Catho-

---

[1] Acts xx. 28.   [2] 1 Peter v. 2.

lic Bishops, that is to say, the Catholic Episcopate, succeeds to the College of the Apostles, and is therefore supreme and infallible, but the Catholic Episcopate includes the Bishop who is pre-eminently the Bishop of Christ's fold, just as the College of the Apostles included the Prince of the Apostles, with each and all of his own personal prerogatives and powers.

The Apostolic Office therefore remains in the Church, in the person of S. Peter's successor, and in the Catholic Episcopate when united to its Divinely constituted Head, the Rock of the whole edifice; for without him there can be no Catholic Episcopate and no succession from the Apostles, according to the mind of Christ. And thus it is not correct to say, as Dr. Oxenham says, that "All Bishops alike are successors of S. Peter *as an Apostle.*"[1]

Nor are the Bishops mere delegates of the Roman Pontiff. This idea is expressly repudiated and condemned by the Church. The Bishops have power and jurisdiction in their own right, for "the Holy Ghost hath placed" them "to rule (feed) the Church of God,"[2] and accordingly the Pope, the Chief Bishop, addresses them as his "venerable brethren." But the actual exercise of that power and jurisdiction which the Bishops hold from God is, by the will of God, united with, and dependent upon, the Apostolic Office, centred and living in the Rock, the chief Ruler,

---

[1] Page 13.  [2] Acts xx. 28.

# INFALLIBILITY

the Chief Shepherd of the whole flock. Hence, he it is who determines the particular portion of the whole flock over which each Bishop is to exercise the powers which he has from the Holy Ghost, because, unlike the individual Apostles, the individual Bishop has not received from God a universal mission in the world,—though even individual Apostles, by their personal gift of universal mission, could not be independent from their Divinely-constituted Head and Prince. A remnant of this principle may be found in the Anglican Church by law Established, in which the Crown, holding jurisdiction over the whole community, names the Bishop in each diocese, and therefore determines the limits within which he is to exercise his powers. The Crown has been substituted for the successor of S. Peter.

## 2—*Infallibility*

The doctrine of the Infallibility of S. Peter and of his successors consists in this, and in this only, that by the special assistance of the Holy Spirit, Who, according to our Lord's promise, is with the Church unto the end of time, the successors of S. Peter inviolably keep and faithfully expound the revelation or deposit of faith delivered through the Apostles. Hence, that when, in the exercise of his Apostolic Office, the successor of Peter speaks as the Chief Shepherd of the whole flock, and expressly declares by what is called a DEFINITION, which he makes known as such, that a doctrine is a revealed doctrine and part of the deposit of the Christian Faith, then, he will not and cannot fall into error. We speak of it as a definition of doctrine regarding FAITH OR MORALS, because the Christian Faith is not merely a speculative doctrine, or system of philosophy, but also, and pre-eminently, a practical one, and it must therefore extend to determine what is a sin and what is not a sin, that is to say, what is contrary to God's Commandments and what is in conformity with those Commandments. And this is the meaning of the term MORALS. It is obvious, then, that in all cases it is a question of doctrine: either of doctrine concerning Christian belief for the Christian mind, or of doctrine concerning the Christian observance of God's Commandments.

Hence Dr. Oxenham may learn, that by Infallibility we do not mean "impeccability" or sinlessness in the person of S. Peter or of his successors, who are accountable to God for their own consciences and their own lives like every other human being; that we do not mean that the Roman Pontiff receives special revelations from heaven, or that by a revelation of the Holy Spirit he may invent or teach new doctrines not contained in the deposit of Faith, though, when occasion offers, and especially in times of conflict, he may define a point which all have not clearly recognised in that Faith, or which some may be striving to put out of view. Nor do we mean that

# INFALLIBILITY

every utterance that proceeds from the Pope's mouth, or from the Pope's pen, is infallible because it is his. Great as our filial duty of reverence is towards whatever he may say, great as our duty of obedience must be to the guidance of the Chief Shepherd, we do not hold that every word of his is infallible, or that he must always be right. Much less do we dream of teaching that he is infallible, or in any degree superior to other men, when he speaks on matters that are scientific, or historical, or political, or that he may not make mistakes of judgment in dealing with contemporary events, with men and things.

Now, upon what grounds do we rest our belief in this prerogative of infallibility thus explained? The answer is: Upon the same grounds as we assert our belief in the supremacy. The infallibility follows necessarily from the supremacy. For, what is the mission of the Church? What is the Church in the world for? To teach the Divinely revealed truth and whatsoever Christ has taught. But how could the Office of S. Peter be instituted by Christ as the Rock of that Church, as the ground of stability in the Divine edifice, if this Rock could be shaken or split up by errors in matters of Faith? How could the edifice stand if that were so? To admit such a possibility is tantamount to saying that our Lord's promise can fail, and that " the gates (powers) of hell," of the father of lies, shall " prevail " against the Church. The Ruler of the Kingdom of heaven would no longer hold the

Keys of that kingdom, if he could open the gateways of error and close the door of revealed truth. The Shepherd would not be feeding the sheep and the lambs with the food of truth, if he could slay them with the poison of erroneous doctrines.

Dr. Oxenham must also learn, together with other Protestants, that we hold all the Apostles to have been infallible, and that they had not to gather from S. Peter the truth which they had been sent to teach. But this infallibility of theirs was their personal prerogative, because it was not given in any other form, and it ceased with their personal mission. Whereas the infallibility of S. Peter, because it was not only personal, but also part of the Office which is essential to the construction of the Church, as the Rock is essential to the edifice which is built upon it, must remain in that Office as long as the Church abides. Nor is it admissible that the supremacy and infallibility of S. Peter depend upon the acceptance or approval of those who were committed to his care to be sustained, to be governed, and to be fed. For the Church was not established after the manner of a Parliament, and if the Rock, the Ruler, and the Shepherd were to be dependent upon the votes or the approval of those who are committed to his care,[1] the whole principle and constitution of the Church established by Christ would be overturned, and the Rock

---

[1] Dr. Oxenham tells us on page 58 of his book that the judgment of the Council of Jerusalem was afterwards endorsed by universal acceptance.

# INFALLIBILITY

would rest on the edifice, not the edifice upon the Rock; the Keys would be in the hands of the subjects, and not under the control of the Ruler; the flock would feed the Shepherd, instead of the Shepherd feeding the flock. Rightly then, and consistently with the texts above mentioned, may the text of S. Luke be quoted to further emphasise the doctrine of the supremacy and infallibility of S. Peter, and it is thus quoted by many of the Fathers, by the Vatican Council, by the present Pope, and by not a few of our theologians: "And thou being once converted, confirm thy brethren."

Let me conclude this paragraph on the infallibility of S. Peter and of his successors, by recalling an argument in its support, which has been so ably suggested by Count J. de Maistre.[1] Once you admit the supremacy, the infallibility follows as a necessary consequence. We have here two different terms which *practically* signify the same thing. For surely in real life, and as far as the *practical* conduct of men is concerned, to be free from error and to be above all possible accusation of error, come practically to one and the same thing. Suppose, for the sake of argument, that no Divine promise had been made to S. Peter and to those who succeed him as the Rock of the Church, the Pope would nevertheless be *practically* infallible, or, what is the same thing, he would have to be considered so, as being the ultimate tribunal

---

[1] Du Pape, BK. I. c. 1, p. 21.

which admits of no appeal. Let the reader reflect, and he will realise that in every social organisation or commonwealth, under any form of government, the judgment of a court that admits of no further appeal is, and must be assumed to be, just and true. It is because that court is supposed to be unerring that it admits of no further appeal, though, of course, not having any Divine assurance, that court in reality may err. Had anyone the right to say that the Pope, who, by virtue of his supremacy, is the ultimate court of appeal in matters of faith, is mistaken, that person would also have the right to disobey him, and this right to disobey him would put an end to the supremacy. For, as we have said, why does a supreme court admit of no appeal if not on the assumption, which is practically enforced, that its judgment is based upon truth, and therefore just? Hence it is that practical infallibility is always asserted as a necessity for the government of every organised society. Surely, then, it must be obvious that in the Church, in the Kingdom of Christ on earth, where the question is not one of mere outward compliance with the law, or of practical government, but one of binding our consciences, of telling us what God wishes us to believe or not believe, surely, I say it must be obvious that infallibility should exist in the Office of the supreme judge, and an infallibility which is not based only upon a necessary assumption for practical purposes, but upon an unassailable and divinely established principle beyond the possibility

# ROME

of mistake. Again, if Christ wished unity of faith to abide in His Church, and He certainly did, He must have provided the proper means of preserving that unity under ordinary and habitual circumstances. A general Council of the whole Episcopate, especially as the Church extends her frontiers, can only be an intermittent and extraordinary means of infallibly proclaiming the truth. We have but to recall the inevitable difficulties which have invariably attended the meetings of every Œcumenical Council in order to realise this. If the personal infallibility of the Chief Shepherd is not admitted, we must conclude that Christ has willed the unity of His Church and yet left her without the means of practically maintaining and preserving it.

### 3—*The Bishops of Rome*

We have dealt with two of the three questions which Dr. Oxenham sets himself to answer on page 12 of his book. We shall have to deal with them again. But we must now turn to the third question which, Dr. Oxenham tells us, involves the double inquiry: (1) " Was it as *Bishop of Rome* that S. Peter held. . . his prerogatives of supremacy and infallibility? Why are we to suppose that these two 'excellent gifts' were given to him as Bishop of Rome, and not as an Apostle? But if S. Peter did not hold these prerogatives *as Bishop of Rome*, why should Bishops of Rome, any more than any other Bishops, succeed to those prerogatives? All Bishops alike are successors of S. Peter *as an Apostle*. (2) And secondly it must be inquired, Was S. Peter ever Bishop of Rome?"[1]

As regards the first question, I should like to point out that Dr. Oxenham has put it into a strange form, so strange that one almost feels inclined to ask him whether he is aware that it was in Cesarea Philippi, and by the Sea of Tiberias, that our Lord spoke to Peter, years before there was any question of his coming to Rome or anywhere else, and that it was in Palestine, and not in Italy, that our Lord lived and conferred powers and prerogatives upon his Apostles. Of course, Dr. Oxenham is aware of this. Then why put such a question? The answer to it, when it is thus worded, is very obvious. Most certainly it was as an apostle that S. Peter received his excellent gifts, yet not as one of the other Apostles, but as their Prince. We have already sufficiently explained this, as the reader may see. Dr. Oxenham appears to attach more importance to the locality than to the office. The successor of S. Peter in his Apostolic and Episcopal office, with whatever special and essential prerogatives were attached to that office, can be no other than the Bishop who succeeded him in the See which he occupied at the time of his death. Had S. Peter died when he was at Antioch, the Bishops of

---

[1] Pages 12-13.

# ROME

Antioch, and not the Bishops of Rome, would have been his successors, and Dr. Oxenham might have called us "Antiochists" instead of "Romanists."

When Dr. Oxenham asks: "Why are we to suppose that these two excellent gifts were given to him (Peter) as Bishop of Rome and not as an Apostle?"— the answer is a very simple one. We are not to suppose any such thing, because S. Peter received those gifts long before he ever set foot in Rome, and as Prince of the Apostles. But he left them to his successors as Bishops of Rome, because it was in Rome that he died, and that he left his office, his episcopate, and its prerogatives.

There remains then only the second point of Dr. Oxenham's double inquiry, which he expresses as follows:—"Was S. Peter ever Bishop of Rome? For, if not, the Popes, *as Bishops of Rome*, are not his successors at all!"[1] I presume that Dr. Oxenham does not intend to question the historical fact of the presence and death of S. Peter in Rome, a fact which all scholars, Catholic and non-Catholic, admit to-day as unquestionable. I need only remind Dr. Oxenham that Lightfoot, Ellicott, Farrar, Westcott, and Gore, Wieseler, Harnack, Hilgenfeld, Renan, Thiersch, and Ewald all acknowledge it as unassailable,[2] and that Lanciani, speaking as an archæologist, declares that it is " established beyond a shadow of doubt by purely

---

[1] Page 13.
[2] See S. Peter in Rome, by A. S. Barnes.

monumental evidence."[1] Let us then consider Dr. Oxenham's question: Was S. Peter ever Bishop of Rome? He replies to it, but in a most perfunctory and superficial manner, on page 108 of his book. We shall have to deal presently with his assertions and arguments put forward in the preceding pages in connection with the text of S. Irenaeus, the General Councils, etc., where he endeavours to show that " it was not the necessities . . . of their position only " which gave the Bishops of Rome their eminence and distinction among other Bishops, but that " it was a matter of express decree, agreed upon by the other Bishops." Here, however, we are concerned only with the question as Dr. Oxenham puts it: Was S. Peter ever Bishop of Rome? The subject is interesting, and for the student of history, a very extensive one, which requires a long and critical examination of evidence. Many modern scholars have discussed it fully, and when Dr. Oxenham consents to take notice of, and to discuss, the existing documents and to reply to the powerful arguments brought forward by recent research,[2] then it will be time enough for me to reply to Dr. Oxenham on this point, as fully as the subject deserves. All I need do here is to deal with what he writes in the hope of convincing his readers that S. Peter was not Bishop of Rome, and

---

[1] Pagan and Christian Rome, p. 123.

[2] Grisar Die Papste des Mittelalters.—Chapman: Revue Bénédictine, 2 Feb., 1895. Duchesne: Les Origines Chrétiennes. Michels: L'Origine de l'Episcopat. Rivington: The Primitive Church and the See of Rome.

# ROME

to sketch the main arguments in support of the Catholic and Roman tradition.

1. The Apostles S. Peter and S. Paul were the FOUNDERS of the See of Rome, and accordingly our calendar, unlike the calendar of the Anglican Church, which only names S. Peter on the feast of June 29th, mentions that feast as the feast of both Apostles; and every Pope issues his most solemn documents with a reference to this glorious tradition. And Tertullian (200 A.D.), S. Cyprian's master, tells us that the Apostles Peter and Paul poured all doctrine (totam doctrinam) into that See,[1] and that Clement, Bishop of Rome, was ordained by S. Peter, though Tertullian by no means excludes the fact that Linus preceded Clement as bishop of that see. S. Peter arrived in Rome in the year 42 A.D., and founded and organised this Church, ordaining priests and deacons. During his temporary absence, the college of Roman priests, under his authority, governed the community. In the year 60 A.D. S. Paul came to Rome, as he had promised to do in his Epistle to the Romans. He was an Apostle, remember, with universal mission, as we have explained above. But S. Peter, as the Rock of the Church and first founder, remained as the first head and Bishop of the See of Rome. I presume that Dr. Oxenham would not attempt to say that there could be two bishops in one see, though it is quite conceivable and consistent with what we have said hither-

---

[1] De Præscr. Hæret. 32.

to of the constitution of the Church that two Apostles should unite in the founding of one see, especially if it was to be the see of the Bishop who succeeded the Apostle and Bishop who was the Rock of the whole Church.

The historical evidence in support of these latter statements is chiefly to be found in the words of S. Clement (90 A.D.), in the words of S. Irenaeus (140-202 A.D.), not to mention other documents old enough to sweep away a number of Dr. Oxenham's arguments. In the earliest and subsequent literature the name of S. Paul is omitted in connection with the "bishopric" of Rome, though it is preserved in connection with the foundation of that see. Eusebius (264-338), for instance, indicates, as we do to-day, the two ways in which those two great Apostles were connected with the see of Rome. Linus, he says,[1] obtained the bishopric of the Church of Rome "first after Peter," and Clement held the "third place of those who acted as bishop after both Paul and Peter."[2] And in his Chronicle,[3] Eusebius writes: "The Apostle Peter, when he had first founded the Church of Antioch, sets out for the City of Rome, and there preaches the gospel, and stays there as *prelate* of the Church for twenty years . . . but he (Peter), besides the Church of Antioch, also first presided over that in Rome until his death."

---

[1] H.E. iii. 4.   [2] iii. 21.

[3] ii. 150.   ὁ δὲ αὐτὸς μετὰ τῆς ἐν Ἀντιοχίᾳ ἐκκλησίας καὶ τῆς ἐν Ῥώμῃ πρῶτος προέστη ἕως τελειώσεως αὐτοῦ.

# ROME

2. Dr. Oxenham ventures to assert that the Clementine Romance,[1] "a pure fiction," is the origin of the story that S. Peter was Bishop of Rome. Now, this is absolutely contrary to fact: (1) Because before the Clementine Romance came into existence, we have the list of the Bishops of Rome made out by Hegesippus, a converted Jew, who came to Rome under Eleutherius, and who drew up that list from the lists already existing, and from the tradition which he found in his time. And again we have the list drawn up by S. Irenaeus and the testimony of Eusebius, which show that the Clementine Romance may have arisen from the previous tradition, but could not have given rise to it. (2) Because there is the famous Epistle of S. Clement, Bishop of Rome, to the Church in Corinth, an epistle described by Irenaeus as "most powerful," and by Dr. Lightfoot as "almost imperious." In that epistle, S. Clement claims divine authority for his right to intervene authoritatively in the dissensions at Corinth, and of calling the riotous faction to order. They are to obey, he says, "the things written by us through the Holy Spirit," and "if any disobey the things spoken by Him through us, let them know that they will involve

---

[1] The Clementine Romance is made up of a narrative which relates how S. Clement met his relations whom he had lost (Recognitions), of certain homilies, and of a letter of S. Clement to S. James. Even Dr. Salmon, one of Dr. Oxenham's greatest authorities, cannot fix the date of the Romance earlier than the "very end of the second century." (Introduction to N. T., p. 14.) It was probably composed much later on in the third century.

themselves in transgression and no small peril." This letter was written during the lifetime of S. John the Apostle. It therefore indicates already at that early date the position and authority of the See of Peter. S. Clement claimed the obedience of the Corinthians. He claimed it from Rome, and it was given and order was restored. The importance and authority of this intervention on the part of the Bishop of Rome, who thus asserted his universal jurisdiction, may be gathered from the words of Denis, Bishop of Corinth, who some seventy years later writes, saying that this letter of S. Clement's was still publicly read in the churches of Corinth, on every Sunday. Nothing of all this could be based upon the Clementine Romance, but it is all remarkably in keeping with the teaching of the Vatican Council "that by the appointment of our Lord, the Roman Church possesses a superiority of ordinary power over all other Churches."[1] (3) Because the Clementine Romance, at all events taken as a whole, is, as Mr. Puller admits, "un-Petrine and un-Roman." Dr. Oxenham therefore must explain how this fiction which even places S. James above S. Peter can be the origin of Papal claims. (4) Because it is most improbable, not to say quite impossible, that men of the stamp of Tertullian and S. Cyprian should have based their ideas regarding the See of Peter upon a Romance. And S. Cyprian in a well-

---

[1] Cap. III. De vi et rat. Prim. Rom. Pont.

# ROME

known passage speaks of the See of Rome as "the Chair of Peter and the principal Church whence sacerdotal unity took its rise."

3. Dr. Oxenham points next to the Isidorian Decretals, as "the great foundation for the exorbitant claims advanced by the mediæval Popes,"[1] and adds that "the edifice of Papal claims . . . has been built up upon this forgery."[2] Well, Dr. Oxenham takes a big leap from the Clementine Romance to the ninth century, and omits to say anything of the documentary evidence supporting Papal claims during the interval of so many centuries previous to the publication of those Decretals. Perhaps this is one of the "important matters" which he felt bound to pass over.[3] Then, why draw the "important" conclusion which is not supported by the premisses? We can afford, however, to take no notice of this omission. The Isidorian Decretals were composed in Western France, not in Rome, about the middle of the ninth century. And in reference to this question we could not do better than quote here what Father Clarke has written in an essay[4] which Dr. Oxenham would do well to read, and from which he may learn much. "Happily," Father Clarke writes, "the False Decretals have had no such influence on the legislation of the Catholic Church. They have introduced no dogma, no law, no custom that did not

---

[1] Page 109. [2] Page 110. [3] Page 108.
[4] The False Decretals, by Father Clarke, S.J.

exist previously. They were never formally recognised by any of the Popes, and it can be proved with certainty that the Holy See knew nothing of them until years after they were compiled, much less had any sort of part in their compilation. If extracts from them occur in some Papal documents, we must remember that they were inserted in perfect good faith, for the authenticity of the False Decretals was widely credited, and at last was taken for granted at Rome itself. The False Decretals were drawn up, as we shall see presently, not in Rome, but in Western France. Their compiler was no member of the Papal Court, but a provincial Bishop, or some one acting under his orders and seeking to advance his cause. Though they go by the name of 'False Decretals,' yet a great portion of them are genuine documents, and those which are forgeries embody the traditional teaching of the Popes whose names are attached to them. They did not introduce even into the discipline of the Church anything that was unknown before, but simply sought to attach the weight of Papal or Conciliar authority to customs which generally prevailed, but which many questioned as lacking any sufficient sanction from the Holy See."

I would remark that for a forgery to be accepted, and to have " undisputed authority for some seven hundred years,"[1] it must indeed bear a great resemblance to truth, and reflect ideas that are pre-

---

[1] Dr. Salmon. The Infal. of the Church, p. 451.

# THE FATHERS 33

valent, or it would deceive no one. And Dr. Oxenham will have to explain how the Isidorian Decretals could be generally welcomed if they did not express what was already a well-rooted belief.

## PART II

### 1—*The Venerable Fathers*

COMMENTING upon a text taken from the writings of S. Cyril of Alexandria, Dr. Oxenham does not hesitate to assert that "at the beginning of the fifth century, the modern Roman doctrine of Papal supremacy was simply unknown."[1] I propose discussing separately the case of each of the great Fathers specially quoted by Dr. Oxenham. But without wearying my readers here with endless references in order to show how this assertion of Dr. Oxenham's is contrary to existing evidence, let me ask them to consider his statement in the light of the texts which I have gathered together in an Appendix to these pages, and they will see that centuries did not pass in the history of the Church "before any single person whose witness has come down to us, ever imagined such a doctrine,"[2] as Dr. Oxenham assures us was the case. "We need no evidence," he writes, "to show that S. Peter had the first place

---

[1] Page 40.  [2] Page 111.

of honour, that he acted as leader and spokesman
of the Apostles on several occasions, that he took
the most prominent place more than once, that he
was truly a 'pillar' of the Church, as also S. James
and S. John are said to have been. No evidence
which proves this is of the smallest value in this
controversy, for all this is freely admitted."[1] It is
very good of Dr. Oxenham to admit so much, though
he fails to see that even in this admission he practically informs us that the Apostles were all the same,
only different. But the texts which we have
collected together, and those which we shall have
occasion to mention in the course of our arguments,
clearly show that the Fathers held S. Peter to be
placed by Christ on a wholly different footing from
all the other Apostles, because He had given to him
all that they had and something more. The reader
may judge for himself.

Nobody needed evidence for what Dr. Oxenham
so freely grants, and the Fathers least of all. Surely
then, it is strange that they should have written so
much to prove what nobody needed evidence to
believe. The fact is that the Fathers taught a great
deal more than Dr. Oxenham admits, and that they
dwelt upon the position of S. Peter and his office
in the constitution of the Church.

We have already explained how all the Apostles,
including Peter, were the foundation of the Church,

---

[1] Page 24.

## THE FATHERS

and how in that sense they were all "pillars." This is freely admitted by all who believe in the special office of S. Peter, the Prince of the Apostles, the "pillar" amongst "pillars." One text from S. John Chrysostom's writings should suffice to open Dr. Oxenham's eyes. "Why then," exclaims that great Father, "did James receive the throne of Jerusalem? This is my answer—That He appointed this man (Peter), not teacher of that throne, but of the habitable world."[1] Mark the words *teacher* and *throne* and *habitable world*, and see what is left of Dr. Oxenham's theory. He admits that S. Peter was the "leader" of the Apostles. But the leader, for what? The Apostles were leaders and teachers and pillars. Undoubtedly, then, he who was the "leader" of those leaders, of those teachers, of those pillars, had a pre-eminent position as teacher and pillar, and, as the Rock of the whole edifice, a position which could only pass away with the Church, and which placed him and those in his office on a wholly different footing to the others. Could Dr. Oxenham have suggested anything more opposed to the spirit and mind of our Blessed Lord than to assign to S. Peter an empty "honour," a position of mere pomp and show, a vain title, a name without authority? Our Saviour never denied that a "first" amongst His disciples and in His kingdom there must be;

---

[1] Hom. 88 in Joan : "Ὅτι τουτον οὐ τοῦ θρόνου, ἀλλὰ τῆς οἰκουμένης ἐχειροτόνησε διδάσκαλον.

He was emphatic as to the principle of authority and gave the "keys" to one; but He repudiated empty honours, vain titles, and first "places" in the Synagogue, as mere "places." He taught that the one who was to be first should act in all humility, following the Master's example, Who indeed was the Master, but acted as the servant of all. He emphasises this teaching when he speaks to Peter, and just as He was telling him that he should confirm his brethren, as if to remind him, more than the others, of the humility with which he should exercise the great authority of his pre-eminent position. And so is it that in conformity with this teaching, the successor of S. Peter calls himself "the Servant of the servants of God." But of mere supremacy of "place" and of "honour," our Lord would have nothing, and nowhere perhaps is that brought out more clearly than in the twenty-second chapter of the Gospel of S. Luke, where our Lord tells us that He prayed so especially for Peter.

### 2—*Maldonatus and Bellarmine*

1. In his second letter to the *Church Times*,[1] Dr. Oxenham irretrievably commits himself to the statement which he has made in his book regarding Maldonatus, and declares once again that this "ultramontane Jesuit doctor acknowledges that three

---

[1] See Preface.

## MALDONATUS

of the greatest doctors of antiquity—Origen, Chrysostom, and Augustine—every one of them differs from modern Romanists,"[1] and that Maldonatus "conclusively refutes the Papal assertions as to the first text on which they rely."[2] Now, I pointed out in my letter that Dr. Oxenham had suppressed the evidence, and I will endeavour to make this clear to the impartial reader. What are the facts? What does Maldonatus really say of the Fathers in connection with the text of S. Matthew?

It is undoubtedly true that Maldonatus begins his commentary with the words quoted by Dr. Oxenham, and that he recalls the fact that some of the Fathers, besides the literal interpretation which they give elsewhere,[3] do interpret the words "super hanc petram" to mean "upon this faith of Peter, or upon this confession of faith by Peter, with which thou hast acknowledged Me to be the Son of God." One of S. Augustine's readings of the text is also given by Maldonatus, and one of Origen's. But here Dr. Oxenham stops short in his quotation from Maldonatus, and thus, as I have said, he suppresses the evidence and entirely misrepresents what Maldonatus really says of the Fathers. Let us see for ourselves. Dr. Oxenham asserts that Maldonatus "goes on, as we might expect, to argue that all those old Fathers were quite mistaken."[4] Maldonatus goes on to do nothing of the sort. For, in the very next sentence

---

[1] Page 26.  [2] Page 32.  [3] See Introductory.  [4] Page 26.

following upon the words quoted by Dr. Oxenham, Maldonatus goes on to write literally thus: "The Calvinists have laid hold of those interpretations taken in a sense different from their meaning, with greater eagerness than with love for truth. . . . We shall interpret the other Fathers a little further on."[1] I am afraid that in this instance Maldonatus would have classed Dr. Oxenham amongst the Calvinists, whom he immediately proceeds to confute at great length by expounding the usual Catholic and obvious interpretation of the text. It is the Calvinists, not those old Fathers, who, he argues, "are quite mistaken," though he does not think that the additional interpretations given by some of the Fathers are easy to reconcile with the literal meaning of the words in S. Matthew's Gospel. And Maldonatus quotes, in support of the well-known reading of the text, Clement of Rome, Hippolitus, Dyonisius, Tertullian, Cyprian, Origen, Epiphanius, Gregory Nazianzen, Basil, Ambrose, Leo, the Council of Chalcedon, Juvencus, and Psellus. And after that he immediately writes as follows:—"Finally, this was the mind of those *very same* Fathers who are brought forward as teaching the opposite." Maldonatus refers us, in support of this latter statement of his, to the writings of those *very same* Fathers, and, having quoted Origen, he names the other Fathers whom he had mentioned before in the

---

[1] Mald. in loco.

# MALDONATUS

passage translated by Dr. Oxenham. S. Hilary (lib. 6 de Trinit.) (in Psal. 131) (can. 16. in Matt.) CHRYSOSTOM. (hom. in Psal. 50.) Cyril. (lib. 2. in Joan. c. 12. 2.) and AUGUSTINE. (serm. 49.) Maldonatus then explains the Retractations of S. Augustine, and then concludes: " From this *it is clear* that the Fathers who said that ' super hanc petram ' was to be interpreted as meaning ' upon this faith,' understood this interpretation differently to heretics. Hence the most correct interpretation seems to me to be that we should say that the Church was built upon the faith and upon the confession of Peter, *i.e.*, upon Peter on account of his faith and confession, as all other authors have held. For we commonly make use of a like phraseology to indicate that the state is founded upon the faith of one man, *i.e.*, upon one man on account of his faith. In the same way S. Ambrose (lib. de Resur. fide.) declared that the faith of Peter, and not his body, walked upon the waters, because, not his body, but his faith made it possible for him to walk upon the waters. Certainly, IT IS MANIFEST FROM THE WORDS OF THESE SAME AUTHORS (FATHERS) THAT THEY DID NOT WISH TO DENY, AS HERETICS DENY, THAT PETER WAS THE FOUNDATION OF THE CHURCH."[1] This is what Maldonatus writes regarding the Fathers mentioned by Dr. Oxenham, and I would ask whether, with the words of Maldonatus before our eyes, words which

---

[1] Mald. *ibid.*

Dr. Oxenham has suppressed, it is true that "Maldonatus acknowledges that all those great doctors of antiquity, and among them three of the greatest—Origen, Chrysostom, and Augustine—every one of them differs from modern Romanists,"[1] or that Maldonatus "conclusively refutes the Papal assertions as to the first text on which they rely."[2] Maldonatus says just the opposite. It is sad no doubt for Dr. Oxenham to find himself classed by Maldonatus among heretics, but he should not have suppressed the evidence, and made out that Maldonatus acknowledges or refutes that which he has neither acknowledged nor refuted. Dr. Oxenham does not like the word "suppress;" and he would rather have me describe his methods as "not reciting." Very well. That is certainly a nice way of putting it, and it is distinctly refreshing to find Dr. Oxenham preferring nice expressions, but the fact remains, and it is an awkward one, that Maldonatus cannot be quoted as admitting that those Fathers "every one of them differs from modern Romanists." And Dr. Oxenham can only uphold that statement by not reciting the evidence which was so much to the point. Like many other Catholic theologians, Maldonatus rightly argues that, whether you interpret "super hanc petram" as meaning "upon Peter" or "upon the faith of Peter," the conclusion is ever one and the same, namely—that upon him did Christ build the Church.

---

[1] Page 26.  [2] Page 32.

# BELLARMINE

2. Bellarmine is another "ultramontane" writer with whose authority Dr. Oxenham endeavours to bolster up his misrepresentation of the teaching of the Fathers upon the supremacy of S. Peter. Bellarmine, we are told,[1] "can quote nothing earlier than the eleventh century, except the suspicious evidence of some Popes in their own cause, of whom the earliest to speak distinctly is Pope Agatho, A.D. 680." Dr. Oxenham is speaking here of the text in S. Luke, "Simon . . . I have prayed for thee," etc. He resorts in this instance to the methods of which I have spoken in my introductory remarks, and therefore changes the whole position. His point was, and is, that all the venerable Fathers did not acknowledge the supremacy and infallibility of S. Peter; whereas here he is simply endeavouring to show that all the Fathers did not agree or prove that doctrine solely on the strength of the one text of S. Luke, a fact which the Pope never thought of denying in the Encyclical now under consideration. Turning, however, to what Dr. Oxenham here says, I would remark:—

1. That it is not a fact that Bellarmine quotes "nothing earlier than the eleventh century, except the suspicious evidence of some Popes in their own cause, the earliest of whom to speak distinctly is Pope Agatho, A.D. 680." For, Bellarmine refers to Leo the Great (serm. 3. de anniv. assumpt.), and

---

[1] Page 33.

Leo the Great lived two centuries before Pope Agatho. Nor can Dr. Oxenham pretend that this Pontiff, whom he describes as a "great champion"[1] of Papal rights, did not speak distinctly upon the prerogatives of S. Peter and of his successors. Not to mention other passages in his writings, in the very homily quoted by Bellarmine, Leo expounds most explicitly the doctrine of the supremacy of S. Peter, and after arguing from the texts of S. Matthew, he adds the texts of S. Luke, as further evidence, just as other Catholic writers usually do.

2. There is nothing suspicious in the evidence of Popes "in their own cause." As the Rev. Spencer Jones, the Anglican Rector of Batsford, points out,[2] "Human nature must be tempted to magnify its office; and it is natural and all for the best that it should have a strong bias in its favour; but it will at least say all that is to be said in its behalf; and on the other hand, where it is a question of government, the first impulse of a subject is to resist authority, and the next is to look about in search for respectable reasons for doing so." It would have been impossible for Leo or any other Pope to assert his authority as he did, and enforce it, an authority of universal jurisdiction, had not that authority been already known as legitimate throughout the world.

3. Bellarmine does not do more than just refer to the text of S. Luke, adding that Greek and Latin

---

[1] Page 106.   [2] England and the Holy See, p. 169.

# BELLARMINE 43

authors (Fathers), have thus interpreted it as further emphasising the supremacy of S. Peter. In the twenty-fifth chapter of his great work, *De Romano Pontifice*, a chapter which is headed, "*Testimony of the Greek and Latin Fathers confirming the primacy of S. Peter*," Bellarmine quotes all the Fathers and doctors of antiquity. The passage mentioned by Dr. Oxenham is but the eighth short paragraph of a chapter in which Bellarmine collects together a considerable number of proofs, as cumulative evidence of what he has already so fully established, and that paragraph is as follows:—" The 8th is in Luke xxii., where the Lord says Simon, Simon satan, etc. By which words the Lord most clearly shows that Peter was to be the Prince and Head of his brethren. Thus are they interpreted by Greek and Latin authors. Theophylactus, speaking of this passage, says:—'Because I hold thee to be the Prince of My disciples, after having wept over thy denial, confirm the others. This is suitable to thee, who, after Me, art the Rock and foundation of the Church.' Leo, in his third sermon, upon the anniversary of his elevation to the Pontificate, comments thus:—'The faith of Peter is specially prayed for, as though the condition of the rest would be more secure, provided the mind of Peter were not subdued.'"[1] Here the passage ends, and Bellarmine goes on to his 9th point. On the strength of this

---

[1] Bellarmine. De Rom. Pontif, lib. I. cap. 20.

short reference, Dr. Oxenham asks us to believe that Bellarmine *could not* quote anything earlier than the eleventh century, and his name is brought forward by Dr. Oxenham in a book in which he has undertaken to show that "all the venerable Fathers" did not acknowledge the supremacy of Peter, and that at the beginning of the fifth century that doctrine was "simply unknown."[1]

### 3—S. Augustine's Retractations

I have given elsewhere[2] the translation of the whole chapter of S. Augustine's Retractations, to which Dr. Oxenham attaches so much importance, and thus my readers will be in a position to judge whether Dr. Oxenham can reasonably make any use of it to strengthen his tottering arguments. "The witness of S. Augustine, even if it stood alone," writes Dr. Oxenham, "is sufficient to prove that Papal assertions as to this text (Matt xvi.) are false. . . . In this book he tells us that when he was young, before he was a Bishop, in explaining the words, 'On this Rock I will build my Church,' he had interpreted 'this Rock' to mean S. Peter; but that afterwards he had preferred (*sic*) another interpretation, and had in 'very many places' in his later writings expounded 'the Rock' to mean Christ Himself; for Christ was 'the Rock,' Whom Simon

---

[1] Page 40. [2] Appendix.

# S. AUGUSTINE

confessing, as the whole Church confesses Him, was called Peter." And to this S. Augustine adds — "But of those two meanings, let the reader choose the more probable."[1] Now, a glance at the full text, which is not given in its entirety by Dr. Oxenham, shows us: (1) that S. Augustine does say in connection with the interpretation of this text, that he wrote upon the subject when he was a priest and before he was a *Bishop*. It is perfectly true that in his preface to the book of Retractations, S. Augustine does allude to what he wrote when he was *young*, as requiring correction; but it is also true that he adds in the same sentence that he does not assume even now that what he is writing will be without blemish. (2) He does not say that he *prefers* a different translation, but only suggests another. (3) He tells us that his great Master and Teacher, "the most blessed Ambrose," gives what Dr. Oxenham would call the "Romanist" interpretation, nor does S. Augustine reject it. He simply says:—" I know that later I have very often explained what our Lord said, 'super hanc petram,' as meaning upon Him Whom Peter confessed, saying, 'Thou art Christ, Son of the living God:' and thus Peter, named after the Rock, typified the Church, which was built upon the Rock and received the keys of the Kingdom of Heaven. FOR IT WAS NOT SAID TO HIM, THOU ART 'PETRA,' BUT 'THOU ART PETRUS.' The Petra

---

[1] Page 28.

was Christ, Whom Simon confessing, as the whole Church confesses Him, was called Petrus. But of these two opinions let the reader choose the more probable."[1]

I might retort to Dr. Oxenham's reasoning,[2] that if S. Augustine had rejected the commonly accepted interpretation given by his great teacher S. Ambrose, he would not have left the reader his choice. Nor could he have left us that choice, in the sense in which Dr. Oxenham takes it, without leaving us free also to hold a doctrine which Dr. Oxenham declares to be an "amazing imposture,"[3] especially as S. Augustine reminds us that Peter received the Keys of the Kingdom of Heaven. But, what is far more important, because it is the point at issue, whichever interpretation S. Augustine may have preferred, he does not retract, or suggest retracting the doctrine of the supremacy of S. Peter, a doctrine which he had repeatedly put forward in his writings, like the other Fathers before him, and in regard to which he leaves us no choice. For example, he writes:—
"Who can be ignorant that the most blessed Peter is the first of the Apostles?"[4] and "Of this Church Peter the Apostle, on account of the primacy of his apostleship, bore the character which represented the whole Church,"[5] and "But I ought rather to fear being contumelious towards Peter. For who

---

[1] Retract. lib. I. c. 21.    [2] Pages 28-29.    [3] Page 112.
[4] Tract. 50 in Joan.    [5] Tract. 124 in Joan.

# S. AUGUSTINE

knows not that that primacy (or princedom) of the Apostleship is to be preferred before any episcopate whatsoever? . . . the possession of that primacy is declared to have been the cause of Peter's having the keys."[1]

But, it may be asked, how was it, then, that S. Augustine could think that such an interpretation of our Lord's words was in any way possible? The answer is given by S. Augustine himself, because, as he says, he was under the impression that "it was not said to him (Peter): Thou art Petra (rock), but Thou art Petrus (Peter)." And here we have the whole explanation. S. Augustine did not know Hebrew or Syriac, a fact which, it would seem, Dr. Oxenham has still to learn. The original text of our Lord's words in the Gospel of S. Matthew places beyond all doubt that our Lord *did* say precisely what S. Augustine thought He had not said, viz.: Thou art Petra (Kephas) and upon this Petra (Kephas),—using in both cases identically the same word. Had S. Augustine known this, it is obvious that he could not possibly have suggested his second reading of the text, because the very reason which he gives to justify it, falls to the ground. There is one conclusion left standing, however, and it is the conclusion that really matters, namely, that S. Augustine, like the other venerable Fathers, acknowledged and taught the supremacy of S. Peter.

---

[1] Enarr. in Ps. 108.

### 4—*S. John Chrysostom*

Few of the Fathers have spoken more explicitly upon the supremacy of S. Peter than S. John Chrysostom, and Dr. Oxenham would have been better advised had he left that great Father of the Greek Church alone. Speaking once again of the text in S. Luke xxii., Dr. Oxenham writes: "If we desire to know what was taught about this text by some of the old Fathers, we may read what S. Chrysostom, in the fourth century, taught. He sees in these words of Christ to Peter no gift of supremacy, or even of superiority, but just the contrary."[1] Dr. Oxenham refers us for this statement of his to S. Chrysostom's 82nd homily on Matt. xxvi. Before explaining the contents of that homily, let us consider Dr. Oxenham's assertion just as it stands: S. Chrysostom "sees in these words of Christ to Peter no gift of supremacy, or even of superiority, but just the contrary." Indeed! Well, then, will Dr. Oxenham kindly read S. Chrysostom's third homily upon the Acts of the Apostles? He will find matter for reflection there, in the following passage: "*And in those days, Peter, rising up in the midst of the disciples, said,* Both as being ardent, and as having had entrusted to him by Christ the flock; as the first of the choir, he always is the first to begin the

---

[1] Page 33.

# S. CHRYSOSTOM 49

discourse. Lo! there were a hundred and twenty; and he asks for one out of the whole multitude. Justly; he has the first authority in the matter, as having had all entrusted to him. FOR TO HIM CHRIST SAID, AND THOU BEING CONVERTED, CONFIRM THY BRETHREN." I fancy that the reader will conclude with me that Dr. Oxenham's statement is plainly false, and that S. Chrysostom does see in *those very words* of Christ to Peter a gift of supremacy, or of superiority, and not just the contrary.

But let us turn to the 82nd homily, from which Dr. Oxenham endeavours to draw an argument against Papal claims. In that homily S. Chrysostom comments upon the events which immediately preceded our Lord's Passion, and expounds various points of Christian doctrine, in the course of which commentary, when he mentions Peter, he calls him the "head" or "summit" of the Apostles. He then dwells at length upon Peter's pride and arrogance in contradicting our Blessed Lord, and is all intent upon teaching the necessity of humility, just as a "modern Papalist" would do, and does constantly to-day, without considering such a commentary "fatal to modern Papal claims."[1] Far from questioning for a moment the supremacy and superior position of S. Peter, which he so repeatedly brings forward, far from seeing "just the contrary" in these words of our Lord, S. Chrysostom proceeds to

---

[1] Page 34.

give, *in the very next sentence* that follows upon Dr. Oxenham's quotation,[1] this most explicit teaching: "Why did He (Christ) not say, I have forgiven, but rather, I have prayed? Because He speaks more humbly as He is about to go to His Passion, in order to manifest His Humanity. For He Who founded and safeguarded the Church upon his (Peter's) confession, so that no danger, nor death itself could overcome him; Who had given to him (Peter) the Keys of the kingdom of heaven, and bestowed upon him such great power, and yet needed not to pray for all these things—how much less should He have needed to pray in this instance? For, indeed, with the greatest authority did He say, I will build my Church [upon *thee*], and I will give to *thee* the Keys of the kingdom of heaven. What necessity, then, was there of prayer in order to sustain the troubled soul of one man? For the reason which we have already ex-

---

[1] "Hear," writes S. Chrysostom, "what He saith: 'I have prayed for thee that thy faith fail not.' For this He said, sharply reproving him, and showing that his fall was more grievous than that of the rest, and needed more help. For the matters of blame were two—both that he contradicted his Lord and that he set himself before the others; and a third fault, namely, that he attributed the fall all to himself. To cure these things, the Lord suffered the fall to take place; and for this cause also, turning from the others, Christ addresses Himself earnestly to Peter, saying, 'Simon! Simon! Satan hath desired to have you, that he may sift *you* as wheat'—that is, that he may trouble, confound, and tempt you—'but I have prayed *for thee*, that thy faith fail not.' And why, if Satan desired *all*, did He not say concerning *all*, 'I have prayed for *you!*' Is it not quite plain that it is this, which I have mentioned before, that it is as *reproving* him, and showing that his fall was more grievous than that of the rest, that Christ directs His words to him." (Quotation by Dr. Oxenham, p. 34.)

# S. CHRYSOSTOM 51

plained, and on account of the weakness of His disciples, who as yet had not an entirely right estimation of Him." And then, after speaking once more of S. Peter's pride, S. Chrysostom concludes with a lesson on humility, and says: "For this reason did He permit the Chief of His Apostles to fall, rendering him more humble, and leading him to greater love. For he is more loved, He said, to whom more is forgiven."[1] These words of S. Chrysostom are fatal to Dr. Oxenham's argument, and he has "not recited" them, though they follow immediately upon the passage which he has quoted. Yes, Dr. Oxenham would have done better to leave S. Chrysostom alone. That great Father has spoken too emphatically to admit of his teaching being questioned. In his Homilies on Penance, he writes: "Peter himself, the Chief of the Apostles, the first in the Church, the friend of Christ . . . this very Peter;—and when I name Peter, I name that unbroken rock, that firm foundation, the great Apostle, the first of the disciples."[2] "And yet after so great an evil [the denial], He again raised him to his former honour, and entrusted to his hand the primacy over the universal Church."[3] And again, not to quote other passages,[4] in his homily on the parable of the Talents, S. Chrysostom calls S. Peter "the leader of the choir of the Apostles, the mouth

---

[1] Hom. 82, on S. Matt. xxvi.     [2] Hom. 3, de Pœn.
[3] Hom. 5, de Pœn.    [4] See my quotation on p. 35.

of the disciples, the pillar of the Church, the buttress of the faith, the foundation of the confession, the fisherman of the universe." May we not name S. Chrysostom, therefore, as one of the Fathers who taught the supremacy of S. Peter?

Even in another passage quoted by Dr. Oxenham, S. Chrysostom's words are significant enough, though Dr. Oxenham endeavours to make him speak only of a first "place," forgetting that the Greek word προστασία is derived from προστάτης (he who presides) and προίσταμαι (to preside, to govern), and is generally translated by the words "presidency," "direction," "government."

### 5—S. Cyril of Alexandria

Little need be said here of the mind and teaching of this Father of the Church, with whose great name Dr. Oxenham strives to dazzle the unwary reader, for Dr. Oxenham gives his own case away in the very text which he quotes, though he does his best to force us to adopt his much-desired conclusion. "If any one asks for what cause Christ asked Simon only, though the other disciples were present, and what he means by 'Feed My lambs' and the like we answer that S. Peter, with the other disciples, had been already chosen to the Apostleship; but because meanwhile Peter had fallen . . . He now heals him that was sick, and exacts a threefold confession in place of his triple denial, contrasting

# S. CYRIL

the former with the latter, and compensating the fault with the correction. For, from what our Lord says, 'Feed My lambs,' a renewal of the Apostolate already delivered to him is considered to have been made, which presently absolves the disgrace of his sin, and blots out the perplexity of his human infirmity."

Let us accept this translation as it is given by Dr. Oxenham. It is false to say that S. Cyril does not teach that our Lord spoke these words to S. Peter alone, "*not* as conferring on him any sort of pre-eminence over others."[1] This is Dr. Oxenham's opinion, not the teaching of S. Cyril. Read over the text and see how S. Cyril tells us that Peter was reinstated by a "renewal of the Apostolate." Exactly so; but not reinstated by halves, or with a diminution of what he had already been promised, but reinstated in the Apostolate *as Christ had described it and bestowed it*, with its special prerogatives and powers, for it was the Apostolate which was Peter's, and he would not have been reinstated had it been diminished.

Now, what was the nature of this Apostolate given to Peter, according to the teaching of S. Cyril? He describes it himself elsewhere. Thus, in his commentary on S. John, he writes: "He (Christ) suffers him no longer to be called Simon, exercising authority and rule over him already as having be-

---

[1] P. 39

come His own. But by a title suitable to the thing, He changed his name into Peter, from the word 'petra' (rock); for on him He was afterwards to found His Church."[1] When "afterwards," if not, according to the meaning of S. Cyril, precisely when Peter was reinstated and Christ said to him: Feed My lambs? And again that great Father writes: "They (the apostles) strove to learn through one, that pre-eminent one, Peter."[2] "And even the blessed Peter, though set over the holy disciples, says, Lord," etc.[3] "If Peter himself, that Prince of the holy disciples, was upon one occasion scandalised," etc.[4]

We might multiply such quotations from the writings of S. Cyril, but surely his teaching is clear in the passages here mentioned.

# PART III

### Arguments from Scripture against the Supremacy and Infallibility

We now come to deal with the latter portion of Dr. Oxenham's book, and first of all with what he is pleased to style the evidence which Holy Scripture affords against the belief in any supremacy or in-

---

[1] T. iv.  [2] *Ib.*, lib. ix.  [3] *Ibid.*  [4] *Ib.*, lib. xii.

# THE ACTS 55

fallibility.[1] He has proved to his own satisfaction that positive Scriptural evidence in support of S. Peter's supremacy and infallibility there is "absolutely none."[2] Here he proceeds to state that there is a considerable body of evidence tending to show that he (Peter) was not supreme nor infallible, confining himself to the evidence afforded by the Book of Acts and Epistles, because, he assures us, that to cite the passages in the life of S. Peter which are recorded in the Gospels is not fair.[3] What a pity that he did not find out sooner that what he was doing up to this point was not fair. He would thus have spared himself, and us, considerable trouble.

(I.)

His first argument is based upon the text, "Ye shall be witnesses unto Me,"[4] because in these words our Lord gave "no sort of superiority to one over another."[5] What Dr. Oxenham can possibly prove from this text is beyond comprehension, except on the supposition that he fails to understand the Catholic doctrine concerning the Apostles, and their relative position to S. Peter. We have already explained that they all received their mission from Christ, and had world-wide powers; and we have also shown that every Catholic (Romanist) believes

---

[1] Page 43.  [2] Page 44.  [3] Pages 44, 45.
[4] Acts i. 8.  [5] Page 45.

this, and that it does not in the least detract anything from the supremacy of S. Peter when that doctrine is properly understood.

Even Dr. Oxenham is obliged to confess that he finds "no positive proof" in this passage of the Book of Acts. *"Meno male!"* as Italians would say.

(II.)

The second argument brought forward by Dr. Oxenham is drawn from the events described in the Acts, in connection with the election of S. Matthias in the place of Judas, the traitor. "They appointed two. . . . But did the supreme and infallible head of the Church choose between these two and appoint the fittest?"[1] exclaims Dr. Oxenham. No; and why should he? What has infallibility got to do with choosing the fittest of these two candidates? And what is there here against the supremacy?

The question was one of special importance, and unique in character. An Apostle had to be elected, that is to say, one who received his mission directly from God. Hence, it became necessary that, as far as possible, God Himself should select the person. Accordingly, the Apostles have recourse to prayer and to a casting of lots. But who undertook the whole matter, which was of such importance? Who declared it to be necessary, and authoritatively placed

---

[1] Page 46.

# THE ACTS

it before the assembled brethren? No other than the Prince of the Apostles. Peter it was who rose up in the midst of the brethren and proved from Holy Scripture the necessity of substituting Judas. He it was who declared that it "must" be done. The Apostles unanimously accepted his declaration, and proceeded to the election. There were no claims of infallibility, nor could there be in such a matter, but there was an act of government on the part of the Prince of the Apostles. Dr. Oxenham does not think so, whereas his friend S. Chrysostom thinks as we do. Listen to the words of that great Father: "Both as fervent, and as one entrusted by Christ with the flock, and as the first of the choir, he ever first begins to speak. . . . But might not Peter by himself have elected? *Certainly;* but he does not so, that he may not seem partial." And, having spoken of the humility of S. Peter, S. Chrysostom points out that there was no abuse of power or proud exercise of authority, though authority there was: "Peter doing this with common consent, nothing with imperiousness, nothing with lordship. . . . He first acts on authority in the matter, *as having himself all put into his hands,* for to him Christ said: And thou, in thy turn, one day confirm thy brethren."[1] The successor of S. Peter would act, and does act, in the same way to-day in all matters of importance, whether of faith or of discipline.

---

[1] Hom. 3 in Act.

(III.)

The institution of Deacons, strange to say, becomes an argument in Dr. Oxenham's hands against the supremacy of S. Peter, because it is written: "The twelve called the multitude of the disciples unto them," and proposed that "seven men of honest report" should be appointed. The proposal "pleased the whole multitude, and they chose Stephen"[1] and the other six. This, we are told by Dr. Oxenham, is "very hard to reconcile with Papal claims."[2] Why? Dr. Oxenham does not say, and who can tell? The twelve Apostles, including Peter, decide to institute the Deacons. The Pope calls together a number of Bishops, and even others who are not Bishops, and together with them decides upon a question, and yet no one dreams of arguing that this is hard to reconcile with the supremacy; much less would any one think of doing so where the twelve Apostles are concerned. But this is Dr. Oxenham's manner of reasoning.

(IV.)

"Now, when the Apostles who were in Jerusalem had heard that Samaria had received the word of God, they sent unto them Peter and John"[3] to confirm those who had already been baptised. "They

---

[1] Acts vi.   [2] Page 48.   [3] Acts viii. 14.

were sent. . . . That was a strange way for the Apostles to deal with that exalted person who was their supreme and absolute ruler!"[1] So writes Dr. Oxenham. This latter exclamation of his amounts almost to a sneer against the person of S. Peter, which, to say the least, is unbecoming. In this fact of the two Apostles being "sent," Dr. Oxenham sees an argument against the supremacy of Peter. Had he considered the whole text of that chapter in the Book of Acts a little more carefully he would have discovered his mistake. For (1) S. Peter was among the *senders*, and hence he may be said to have *sent* himself, especially as he always took the lead. (2) There is no objection to those who are in a subordinate position expressing their wish that their superior should act in a given way, nor in their "sending" him. This is all the more intelligible where Apostles are concerned. Nations, before now, have "sent" their Sovereigns and Princes on important missions, without suggesting a doubt as regards their superiority. And to only mention instances taken from Holy Scripture, has Dr. Oxenham forgotten what we read in the Old Testament,[2] that the people of Israel "sent" Phinees, the son of Eleazar the priest, and ten *princes* with him, to the Rubenites? Will Dr. Oxenham question the position and authority of Phinees and of the ten Princes, because they were "sent"? Again, we read that Paul and Barnabas

---

[1] Page 49.    [2] Josue xxii. 13.

were sent to Jerusalem by the Antiochians to consult the Apostles.[1] Are we to conclude that Paul was their equal or their inferior, or not an Apostle because they sent him? (3) If Dr. Oxenham will refer to the whole narrative in the chapter of the Acts which he has mentioned, he will find that S. John is simply S. Peter's companion, and that he acts the second part. Peter it was who proclaimed the teaching, and he alone commands, judges, condemns, and finally inflicts punishment upon Simon Magus. Dr. Oxenham remarks: "Let us try to imagine an ecclesiastical assembly in mediæval or in modern Rome 'sending' the Pope and some other Bishop down to Naples, or elsewhere, to hold a confirmation."[2] Well, the idea is picturesque, but it is not inadmissible if Dr. Oxenham will also imagine the Pope in Italy with only a few Bishops round him to provide for all the needs of the Church. In such circumstances, the Pope might very easily be "sent" down to Naples, or elsewhere, to hold a confirmation, and when he got there he might condemn another Simon Magus. "S. Peter," says Dr. Oxenham, "appears to have gone to Samaria, when he was *sent* without exhibiting any consciousness that his dignity was injured."[3] Yes, because his dignity was not injured, nor had S. Peter the proud and over-sensitive nature which Dr. Oxenham seems to think necessary in one who holds an exalted office. That is all.

---

[1] Acts xv. 2.     [2] Page 49.     [3] *Ibid.*

# THE ACTS

(v.)

We are now invited by Dr. Oxenham to see another argument against the supremacy and infallibility of S. Peter in the description of an event narrated in the Acts,[1] which, as a matter of fact, when it is not garbled and misrepresented, sets forth the position and authority of S. Peter in a most remarkable way. It is no other than the conversion of Cornelius and his household, an event, which, as Dr. Oxenham rightly remarks, was "a most notable" one, and "fraught with immense results; for it was the declaration that the religion of Jesus Christ was not a limited or racial religion, like the religion of the Jews, but that it was essentially, what it has ever professed to be, a Catholic religion, for all nations alike, for every country, and for every age."[2] He might have added, and therefore not a national branch religion.

Consistently with his method of "not reciting," Dr. Oxenham only recalls the events narrated in the eleventh chapter of the Acts, without a word upon what we are told in the tenth chapter, though that chapter is so essentially connected with all that follows in the eleventh chapter, that it cannot be separated from it. We must ask the reader to consider these two important chapters together, and see for themselves what they relate.

---

[1] Acts x., xi.　　[2] Page 50.

God sent an Angel to Cornelius, but Peter, and not the Angel, is chosen by God to declare the supremely important doctrine of the preaching of the Gospel to the Gentiles. He alone, who was the Rock, the Ruler, and the Shepherd of the whole flock, is selected by God to receive the great revelation, in preference to all the other Apostles, and in spite of their all having been commissioned to teach all nations. This of itself already constitutes a most striking proof of S. Peter's position. Peter in an "ecstasy of mind" receives the great vision, as it were, of a "great linen sheet let down by the four corners from heaven to the earth, wherein were all manner of four-footed beasts and creeping things of the earth and fowls of the air." "God hath shewed *to me*," he was able to say, "to call no man common or unclean."[1] Accordingly, Epiphanius, in the fourth century, writes that the mission of bringing the Gentiles into the Church was bestowed upon all the Apostles, "but most of all on blessed Peter."[2] Peter, to whom the care of the whole flock had been given, was thus told what the extension of Christ's fold was to be, embracing within its limits Jews and Gentiles, without distinction.

And here we come to Dr. Oxenham's extraordinary argument. On Peter's return to Jerusalem, "the Apostles and brethren who were in Judea, having heard that the Gentiles also had received the word of God . . . they that were of the circumcision con-

---

[1] Acts x.  [2] Hœr. 28, 3.

… tended with him."[1] And we are told what they said. "Why didst thou go in to men uncircumcised and didst eat with them?" A very natural question, it would seem, for those to put, who as yet were not aware of the full design of God's providence, as Peter now was. Dr. Oxenham concludes that those who *contended* with him were "evidently altogether unconscious that he was their supreme ruler, and infallible in all his judgments on matters of faith and morals."[2] Does Dr. Oxenham hold, then, that the Apostles were not infallible in their judgments on matters of faith and morals, or deny that Peter was at all events one of the infallible Apostles, to say the least? It would appear so, by this remark. It is quite possible that those who were of the circumcision in those early days were unconscious of a great many things which they had yet to learn, but there is not the slightest evidence here against the supremacy and infallibility of S. Peter. When holy Job said: "If I did despise the cause of my manservant or of my maidservant, when they *contended* with me,"[3] did he imply that his servants were his equals or "altogether unconscious" of the fact that he was their lord and master? S. Peter, in reply to the question addressed to him, proceeds at once to relate his great vision and to explain the revelation, and he does so with such authority that all "held their peace and glorified God, saying, God then has also to the Gentiles given repen-

---

[1] Acts xi.     [2] Page 50.     [3] Job xxxi. 13.

tance unto life."[1] Dr. Oxenham discovers in this event a proof against the supremacy and infallibility of S. Peter, and says that he *submitted* his case to the assembly, as if their approval, and not his authority in declaring his vision, really settled the matter. A more foolish travesty of the facts narrated in the Book of Acts one could hardly conceive. And, awkwardly enough for Dr. Oxenham, here again is his friend, S. Chrysostom, contradicting his views. After stating that " not the Apostles, but those that were of the circumcision " contended with Peter, S. Chrysostom expresses at great length his admiration for S. Peter's humility, bringing forward, as he does, God's direct action in the matter and not his own, and then he exclaims : " See how he defends himself, and will not use his dignity as the teacher, for he knew that the more gently he spoke with them, the surer he was to win them."[2] And the great S. Gregory thus comments upon the incident: " And yet the same first of the Apostles, filled with so great a grace of gifts, supported by so great a power of miracles, answers the complaint of the faithful by an appeal, not to authority, but to reason. . . . For if, when blamed by the faithful, he had considered the authority which he held in holy Church, he might have answered that the sheep entrusted to the shepherd should not venture to censure him. But if, in the complaint of the faithful, he had said anything of his own power, he would

---

[1] *Ib.*  [2] In Act. Ap. hom. 24.

not have been the teacher of meekness. Therefore he quieted them with humble reason, and in the matter where he was blamed even cited witnesses. If, therefore, the Pastor of the Church, the Prince of the Apostles, having a singular power to do signs and miracles, did not disdain, when he was censured, humbly to render account, how much more ought we sinners, when blamed for anything, to disarm our censurers by a humble defence."[1] Dr. Oxenham fails to see the difference between authority and the use of authority, and the lesson of Peter's humility escapes him.

(VI.)

The Council of Jerusalem is the next notable event related in the Acts which affords Dr. Oxenham a proof, as he thinks, that S. Peter was neither supreme nor infallible. The matter under consideration is obviously connected with the point which we have just been discussing. The mere fact, however, of the assembling of a Council, constitutes, in Dr. Oxenham's eyes, an argument against the supremacy and infallibility. Because S. Peter does not use his authority imperiously, and once more gives us an example of wisdom and humility, acting nevertheless with very great power, Dr. Oxenham concludes against the existence of Peter's prerogatives. The Acts narrate that: "the Apostles and ancients

---

[1] Lib. ix., Ep. 39.

assembled to consider of this matter."¹ "But what was the good of all these men considering the matter," exclaims Dr. Oxenham, "if one among them knew infallibly what ought to be done? And if, moreover, he was authorised and empowered as the Vicar of Christ to impose his supreme decision upon the whole Church?"² The answer is not difficult to give, and has already been suggested to us by S. Chrysostom in the previous instance—because the supremacy and infallibility of S. Peter do not imply that he, nor any of his successors, is to use his prerogatives like a tyrant, or after the manner of some magic talisman to be hurled at the Church on every occasion without reason, or without consultation with those who have a mission of teaching together with him.

But what are the facts, as they are described in the text of the Acts? Dr. Oxenham declares that S. James presided over the Council of Jerusalem.³ Where are his proofs for this statement? Nothing of the kind is said in the Book of Acts, and Dr. Oxenham is obliged to confess that "We are not told in the narrative of the Book of Acts the reason why S. James presided."⁴ No, of course not, considering that we are not told that S. James presided at all, and that Dr. Oxenham has invented this for himself. To say that S. James must have presided because he was Bishop of Jerusalem, either then or later, is beside the point and simply to beg the whole question.

---

[1] Acts xv. [2] Page 53. [3] Page 53. [4] Page 54.

# THE ACTS 67

Now, the description of what took place at the Council of Jerusalem, as we read it in the Acts, is totally different to the one with which we are favoured by Dr. Oxenham. For we read there that S. Peter was the first to rise up and address the assembled brethren, who, as we may rightly presume, waited for him to speak. He proceeded forthwith to make the following most solemn declaration of *his* election by God to the privilege of receiving the Gentiles. Listen to his words: " Men brethren, you know that in former days God made choice among us that *by my mouth* the Gentiles should hear the word of the gospel, and believe. And God who knoweth the hearts," etc.[1] S. Peter therefore declares that God has already manifested what the decision is to be, and by *his* ministry. He accordingly goes on to exclaim with words full of power : " Now, therefore, why tempt you God to put a yoke upon the necks of the disciples, which neither our fathers or we have been able to bear? But by the grace of the Lord Jesus Christ we believe to be saved, in like manner as they also."[2] And what was the result of these words of authority, upon the Jewish converts who felt so strongly in regard to the matter? The text tells us that " all the multitude held their peace." Most distressing it is for Dr. Oxenham, but unfortunately S. Chrysostom contradicts him once again. " How full of power," writes this great Father, " are the words (of Peter);

---

[1] Acts xv. 8.  [2] Acts xv. 10, 11.

he says here what Paul has said at great length in the Epistle to the Romans. . . The seeds of all this lie in Peter's discourse. . . See, he first permits a discussion to arise in the Church, and then he speaks."[1] After S. Barnabas and S. Paul, S. James addresses the assembly, and how does he begin his argument? He immediately refers to Peter's words, not to the words of either Barnabas or Paul. "Simon," he says, "hath related how God first visited to take of the Gentiles a people to his name."[2] He thus emphasises all that Peter had declared God to have done "by his mouth." And then S. James expresses his own judgment in full conformity with Peter's declaration. Why should he not have done so? What is there inconsistent here with the true conception of Peter's office as Prince of the Apostles? S. James was his fellow-apostle. Though in union with, and in a measure dependent upon Peter, S. James was a teacher and a judge in Council, and he gave his judgment, just as every Bishop must do, and has done, in every Œcumenical Council under the supremacy of the Pope. It would appear from Dr. Oxenham's manner of reasoning that the head of an assembly, who takes the initiative and declares the course to be pursued by those who are sitting in judgment with him, loses his prerogatives by the mere fact of other judges being present and rising up to express their mind. For, it was *his own* sentence that S. James gave. Dr. Oxenham actually

---

[1] Hom. 32.   [2] v. 14.

# THE ACTS

dares to change the words of Holy Writ and say that
" S. James rose and gave *the sentence of the Council*."[1]
That is absolutely contrary to the narrative in the
Acts. The text distinctly asserts that S. James said:
" Wherefore *my sentence* is———," or as we have it *I
judge*. The SENTENCE of the COUNCIL is given much
further on in verse 28, as follows: "For it hath
seemed good to the Holy Ghost and to us, to lay no
further burden upon you than these necessary
things: that you abstain from things sacrificed to
idols, and from blood, and from things strangled, and
from fornication, from which things keeping yourselves, you shall do well. Fare ye well." This is
the Decree and Judgment of the Council of Jerusalem,
with Peter at its head; a decree common to all judges
in the category in which each one is placed. Nor may
one travesty the narrative by saying that it implies
that all the judges were of equal rank. Therefore is
it that S. Jerome, in the fourth century, writes that
Peter " used his wonted freedom, and that the Apostle
James followed his sentence, and all the ancients at
once acceded to it, and the decree was drawn up
on his wording."[2]

To be logical, Dr. Oxenham must go further and say
that the Ancients and Brethren had the same rank
and authority as the Apostles, because the decree of
the Council of Jerusalem was issued as the decree of
" the Apostles, Elders, and Brethren." Will he dare

---

[1] Page 54.    [2] Ep. 75 int. August.

to say this? We hardly think so. And yet when he is intent upon inveighing against the supremacy of S. Peter, he does not shrink from such reasoning.

(VII.)

The case of Ananias and Saphira, and S. Peter's remarkable and most significant exercise of authority in connection with the sin of those two unfortunate souls is not mentioned by Dr. Oxenham, but he, of course, lays hold, with much eagerness, of the famous incident recorded in the Epistle to the Galatians, when S. Paul rebuked S. Peter. It was not likely that Dr. Oxenham would fail to try and make capital out of that notable event, in support of his contention, as so many Protestants have done before him, wresting the text "as they do also the other Scriptures to their own destruction."[1] Dr. Oxenham, as we have remarked before,[2] gives proof here that he has not understood the nature of the prerogative of infallibility which is claimed for S. Peter and for his successors, and very little, too, of the supremacy. Had he understood what we mean by infallibility, he could never have written the following sentence: "For whether S. Peter's fault on this occasion were one 'of faith' or 'of fact,' whether his fault were 'light and venial' or not, the fact remains that he was in the wrong, that S. Paul withstood him before the

---

[1] 2 Pet. iii., 16.   [2] See Introductory chapter.

# THE ACTS

Church, and openly rebuked him."[1] Now, we have explained elsewhere what is meant by infallibility, and the reader will see at a glance that in order to prove anything against this prerogative of S. Peter, the point which Dr. Oxenham had to establish, was precisely that S. Peter's fault on that occasion was one "of faith." That is the kernel of the whole question, unless the true meaning of *infallibility*, as taught by Catholics, is misrepresented and made to signify something very different to that which is really claimed for S. Peter and for his successors. Dr. Oxenham has not proved the point that concerns us in this controversy, and he could not do so.

But what was the reason of S. Paul's rebuke and the subject of discussion? The facts are clearly before us. S. Peter was blamed by S. Paul for what he *did*, and not for what he *taught*. He was rebuked because "before that some came from James, he did eat with the Gentiles, but when they were come, he withdrew and separated himself, fearing them who were of the circumcision."[2] It was therefore not his faith, but his manner of acting which S. Paul thought it necessary to censure under the circumstances. Precisely because Peter occupied such a pre-eminent position, his behaviour influenced others, and influenced them in a way which might hamper the conversion of the Gentiles, with whom S. Paul was so especially dealing. And it was on account of S.

---

[1] Page 58.   [2] Gal. ii. 12.

Peter's pre-eminent position that S. Paul attached such great importance to S. Peter's behaviour. S. Chrysostom tells Dr. Oxenham this: " If it had been another Peter," he writes, " his change would not have had such power as to draw the rest of the Jews with him. For he did not exhort or advise, but merely dissembled and separated himself, and that dissembling and separation had power to draw after him all the disciples, on account of the dignity of his person."[1] The Jewish practices, that were not incompatible with the New Law, were not forbidden, and were permitted to the Jewish converts, who clung very naturally to many of their old traditions. On the other hand, they constituted a yoke which was not to be imposed upon the Gentiles, as S. Peter, speaking of the doctrinal principle, had clearly declared at the Council of Jerusalem. Whether or not S. Peter was really at fault in acting in two different ways, according to his manner of appreciating the circumstances, the fact is that when he was with the Gentiles, " before that some came from James, he did eat with the Gentiles,"[2] and when those Jews did come from James, he feared displeasing or scandalising them, and acted according to their custom, a custom which, presumably, was allowed by S. James. Has Dr. Oxenham forgotten that S. Paul, when he thought that the circumstances justified his doing so, acted precisely on

---

[1] Hom. in loc.     [2] Gal. ii. 12.

# THE ACTS

the same principle? Let Dr. Oxenham consider the two texts which I have here placed side by side.

| Galatians ii. 3. | Acts xvi. 3. |
|---|---|
| But neither Titus, who was with me, being a gentile, was compelled to be circumcised. | And taking him (Timothy) he circumcised him, because of the Jews who were in those places. For they all knew that his father was a gentile. |

Here we have S. Paul, out of regard for the Jews, not merely eating according to the Jewish custom, but actually obliging his disciple Timothy to be circumcised, because he was the " son of a Jewish woman that believed, but his father was a Gentile." The fact of Timothy's father being a Gentile, and his mother a Jewish convert was not sufficient in S. Paul's eyes to dispense with the rite of circumcision, " because of the Jews who were in those places." Whereas, in other circumstances, he did not compel Titus to be circumcised. It was on the same principle that S. Peter acted in Antioch, eating with the Gentiles, in one instance, and separating himself in the other. S. Paul, however, did not consider that the circumstances at Antioch were such as to allow of Peter acting in this way. The two Apostles therefore took a different view of those circumstances. Hence the rebuke. But what has this to do with infallibility? And as to S. Peter's supremacy, a little attention suffices to show that the whole tenor of S. Paul's argument to the Galatians, who had calumniated him, constitutes a fresh indication of the supremacy which he acknowledged in S. Peter. For, the force of his reasoning lies precisely in this, that he had resisted *even* Peter, and blamed his conduct at Antioch, thus placing beyond doubt that he could not be accused of considering the "works of the Law" as necessary in the Law of Christ. S. Paul could not fail to convince his accusers when he showed them that he had not hesitated to protest on one occasion *even* against Peter's condescension towards the Jews. And Peter, as they knew, held the most exalted position.

Does Dr. Oxenham imagine that even to-day a Bishop might not expostulate with a Pope, who, in his judgment, might be acting in a way which was liable to mislead those under his own charge, and then write to his critics that he had not hesitated to pass strictures upon the action of the successor of S. Peter? The hypothesis is quite conceivable, and in no way destroys or diminishes the supremacy of the Pope. And yet an individual Bishop does not occupy the exceptional position of S. Paul, a fellow-Apostle of the Prince of the Apostles. Even a humble nun, S. Catherine of Siena, expostulated with the reigning Pontiff, in her day, whilst fully acknowledging all his great prerogatives.

We may conclude this argument with another text from S. Chrysostom, who again steps in to refute Dr. Oxenham's views about S. Peter. "Observe his (Paul's) prudence," writes that Father of the Greek Church, "he said not to him (Peter), thou dost wrong in living as a Jew, but he alleges his (Peter's) former

# THE ACTS 75

mode of living, that the admonition and the counsel may seem to come, not from Paul's mind, but from the judgment of Peter already expressed. For, had he said, thou dost wrong to keep the Law, Peter's disciples would have blamed him, but now, hearing that this admonition and correction came, not from Paul's judgment, but that Peter himself so lived, and held in his mind this belief whether they would or not, they were obliged to be quiet."[1]

Dr. Oxenham concludes his paragraph with a further misrepresentation, which is remarkable. He adds: "and the subsequent judgment of the Church, first formulated by the Council at Jerusalem, and afterwards endorsed by universal acceptance, declared that S. Paul was in the right."[2] These words imply surely that the decree of the Apostles, sitting in Council at Jerusalem, was not authoritatively delivered, in spite of the Apostles saying that it had seemed good " to the Holy Ghost " and to them, and that it required to be endorsed by universal acceptance. Where will Dr. Oxenham stop? However, considering that S. Peter was at the Council of Jerusalem, and formulated the judgment, and that he was the first to formulate it, the conclusion must be that S. Peter "declared that S. Paul was in the right." How is this to be used as an argument against S. Peter's supremacy and infallibility?

And now Dr. Oxenham gives us a most alarming

---

[1] Hom. in loc.   [2] Page 58.

piece of news under the sensational heading: "S. PETER DISAPPEARS!"[1] The heading might have been taken from the *New York Herald* or from the *Daily Mail*, and when I read it, it was with some anxiety that I hastened to ascertain whether Dr. Oxenham had discovered that S. Peter had been kidnapped, or that something equally dreadful had befallen the great Apostle. Happily, there is no cause for alarm. Dr. Oxenham only wishes to inform us that the Book of Acts, after having spoken of S. Peter in the course of fifteen chapters, and having said all that it had to say about him, does not say any more. A most astonishing fact!

(VIII.)

After all that we have repeatedly said, in the preceding pages, of the nature of the Apostolic mission, of the relative position of the Apostles to their Prince and Head, and of the difference between individual Bishops and the Apostles with their personal prerogatives, not much is required now to dispose of Dr. Oxenham's attempt to argue against S. Peter's very special and abiding prerogatives, from the Epistles of S. Paul. Dr. Oxenham's opening remarks on page 59 of his book strike one as somewhat contradictory. "*Nowhere*," he writes, and the italics are his, " in the record of S. Paul's Apostolic journeys does he make mention that he is acting under the direction, or even

---

[1] Page 58.

# S. PAUL

by the advice or consent of S. Peter." But Dr. Oxenham goes on to say in the very next sentence, where he speaks of S. Paul going to visit S. Peter, that nothing could be more natural than that S. Paul should have gone to "take counsel" with S. Peter, and that "Such a visit seems to imply that S. Paul at that time regarded S. Peter as one whose experience and *advice* might be useful."[1] This remark leaves us to wonder whether S. Paul, according to Dr. Oxenham's view, did or did not take counsel with S. Peter; or whether Dr. Oxenham thinks that S. Paul went to "take counsel" with S. Peter with his mind made up not to act in conformity with the advice that he received. Many people, no doubt, follow that course, but we can hardly admit that S. Paul so acted.

As to what Dr. Oxenham writes in this chapter, his arguments are so far beside the mark, that it will suffice to recall to mind the following points. (1) S. Paul, being an Apostle, and having therefore received his mission directly from Christ, was not called upon to appeal for direction to S. Peter, though he could never act inconsistently with Peter's special prerogatives bestowed also by Christ, or, in that sense, without dependence upon the office of Chief Shepherd, which Christ had instituted in the Church long before S. Paul's conversion. (2) S. Paul, as regards the Apostolate, was indeed not " behind the very chiefest

---

[1] Page 59.

of the Apostles," as he himself tells those of the Corinthians and Galatians who were inclined to question his apostolic mission and authority, and harboured the prejudice that they were less favoured because S. Paul was not sent forth by Christ under the same circumstances as the other Apostles. The very fact, however, of comparing himself in this respect with the "very chiefest of the Apostles" indicates that he was not inferior to them as regards the apostolic mission, while it implies that there could be a difference of rank even amongst the Apostles, and hence does not exclude the special position of one of them, if that position was known to exist. (3) Having received his mission from Christ Himself, S. Paul had not to appeal to the authority of Christ's Vicar, but to what he himself had preached by Christ's authority. "For neither did I receive it of man, nor did I learn it; but by the revelation of Jesus Christ."[1] (4) S. Paul could teach everywhere in all the Churches, like every one of the Apostles, and especially in the Churches which he had founded. All these things we freely admit and most emphatically teach, nor are they in the least incompatible with the true conception of supremacy and infallibility in S. Peter. Dr. Oxenham endeavours to make a point out of one solitary text[2] in which S. Peter does not happen to be mentioned first. He forgets the almost innumerable texts in which S. Peter is most markedly spoken of

---

[1] Gal. i. 12.    [2] Gal. ii. 9.

before the others, and which prevent us from drawing any conclusion from the order in which the three Apostles happen to be mentioned in this one instance. Moreover, Dr. Oxenham does not remember that several ancient manuscripts of this very text do name Peter first. The original Latin version does so, and this reading is accepted by Tertullian, Chrysostom, Ambrose, Augustine, Jerome, Irenæus, Gregory of Nyssa, and others. We need not stop to dwell further upon S. Paul's testimony to the office of S. Peter, and we have said enough to be able to conclude that Dr. Oxenham cannot prove that "the language and the conduct of S. Paul . . . are uniformly and unmistakably fatal to the Papal pretension that S. Peter was either infallible or supreme."[1]

(IX.)

Passing on to discuss the two Epistles of S. Peter, Dr. Oxenham has very little to say about them, and he is content simply to assert that they compel us to choose between two alternatives—(1) "Either S. Peter was really unconscious of being supreme and infallible; or (2) he managed to conceal his consciousness of this momentous truth in a manner which must have been sadly misleading to those whom he was bound to teach and to guide aright, in a manner which was scarcely consistent with honesty or with charity—if

---

[1] Page 63.

being conscious of this great truth, and knowing its immense importance, he nevertheless concealed it."[1] Such is Dr. Oxenham's way of reasoning. Why we are to believe that S. Peter only taught and wrote what is contained in these two very short Epistles, the only ones which are preserved to us, Dr. Oxenham does not say. It is obvious that he taught a great deal more, though there was no necessity for him to speak in these two Epistles of every doctrine of which he was fully conscious.

According to Dr. Oxenham's manner of reasoning, we might assert that S. Peter was unconscious, or that he concealed his belief in many momentous doctrines, of which Christ spoke, because S. Peter does not happen to refer to them in his two Epistles. Surely this is sophistry, if anything is, and it requires only to be pointed out to be dismissed with a smile. On such grounds it would be quite easy a hundred years hence to convict Dr. Oxenham of being unconscious, or of concealing the mysteries of Christian Faith, and a number of other truths which are not mentioned in his book. As a matter of fact, however, the opening sentence of S. Peter's first Epistle, written, as it was, in Rome, is particularly significant, and suggests, to say nothing more, that he was conscious of his supreme authority. Listen to his words : " Peter, an apostle of Jesus Christ to the strangers dispersed through Pontus, Galatia, Cappadocia, Asia, and Bythinia, elect."

---

[1] *Ibid.*

# TRADITION

Here we have whole regions mentioned in which Peter exercises his universal jurisdiction, and regions in which the Apostles were still preaching. That sentence reminds us of S. Chrysostom's comment upon S. Peter's inspection of all the Churches, mentioned in the Acts ix., 32, and with those words of S. Chrysostom we may conclude this paragraph: "Like a general he went round surveying the ranks, seeing what portion was well massed together, what in order, what needed his presence. Behold him making his rounds in every direction."[1]

## PART IV

### (I.)

#### THE CONSTANT BELIEF OF EVERY AGE

POPE LEO XIII., in his Encylical on the *Unity of the Church*, after touching upon the arguments and testimony of the Fathers and Doctors of the Church, on behalf of the supremacy of S. Peter and of his successors, concludes with these words: "Wherefore, in the decree of the Vatican Council as to the nature and authority of the primacy of the Roman Pontiff, no newly conceived opinion is set forth, but the venerable and constant belief of every age."[2] These words furnish Dr. Oxenham with an opportunity of making a fresh onslaught, and in his fourth and fifth lectures

---

[1] Hom. 21 in Act.     [2] Satis cognitum, page 56.

he strives to overturn the Pope's conclusion by assertions which become bolder as he proceeds. Referring once again to the texts of Holy Scripture, he assures us " that we have seen that the venerable Fathers are not at all agreed as to those texts, except in one point, namely, that no one of them (*sic*) interprets either of those texts as the Church of Rome does."[1] That this statement is utterly wide of the truth hardly requires further evidence, and the passages which we have quoted from the writings of the Fathers, together with those which we have collected in our Appendix, are surely sufficient to show that Dr. Oxenham ignores the existing evidence and that he is trading upon the credulity of his readers. There is a great deal, therefore, in these two last lectures of Dr. Oxenham's which does not demand further attention, and that we need not revert to again. However, as some of the assertions contained in the latter portion of his book are particularly bold, and by their very boldness may impress the minds of certain people, we cannot pass them over without a few remarks.

" SILENCE OF THIRTEEN CENTURIES " is the startling heading under which Dr. Oxenham begins this next attack upon Papal claims, but in support of his contention he prudently refrains from quoting more than two sentences of Döllinger's work, " *The Pope and the Council.*" To this assertion we may immediately oppose what Renan writes, and we presume

---

[1] Page 66.

# TRADITION 83

that Dr. Oxenham will not go the length of describing Renan as an advocate of Roman claims. "Rome," he says, "was the place in which the great idea of Catholicity was worked out. More and more every day it became the capital of Christianity, and took the place of Jerusalem as the religious centre of humanity. Its Church claimed a precedence over all others, which was generally given. All the doubtful questions which agitated the Christian conscience came to Rome to ask for arbitration, if not decision. . . . At the end of the second century we can already recognise by signs which it is impossible to mistake the spirit which in 1870 will proclaim the Infallibility of the Pope. . . . Irenaeus (lib. iii. 3.) refutes all heresies by reference to the belief of this Church—the greatest, the oldest, the most illustrious—which possesses in virtue of unbroken succession the true tradition of the Apostles Peter and Paul, and to which, because of its primacy, all the rest of the Church ought to have recourse."[1] So writes one as prejudiced and unbelieving as Renan, and yet Dr. Oxenham would have us accept his assertion that "there was no mention ever made of that important truth,"[2] that there was no trace of it during thirteen centuries, and that "it was denied and rejected as soon as it was advanced."[3]

Dr. Oxenham nevertheless seems almost afraid of

---

[1] Hibbert Lecture for 1880. Eng. translation, pages 172-174.
[2] Page 67. [3] Page 74.

his own statement, and no wonder! For he immediately drops his "thirteen centuries" and proceeds to argue that there was a silence of only four hundred years; and even there he feels unsafe, and takes refuge in three centuries. "In Holy Scripture," he writes, "it is not recorded that S. Peter assumed to decide, by his supreme and infallible authority, any question of faith or morals. It is recorded that such questions arose, and it is recorded how they were settled, but they were not settled by S. Peter."[1] Now, we have seen that Holy Scripture does speak of S. Peter's most authoritative action in the early days of the Church, at the Council of Jerusalem, and we have reminded our readers of other instances of the exercise of his supreme authority in the case of Ananias and Saphira, of Simon Magus, etc., and of his special visitation and inspection of the Churches founded by others. Little indeed there could be in Scripture of the exercise of Peter's authority in the initial stages of the Apostolic preaching during the lifetime of the other Apostles, and before the Church had fully developed her organisation throughout the world. There is more than we might have expected, and what is said is already a great deal. Nor does Dr. Oxenham undertake to show us that a more frequent and explicit exercise of S. Peter's authority was called for under the circumstances, and in the judgment of S. Peter

---

[1] Page 68.

himself. And surely S. Peter, and not Dr. Oxenham, could judge when, and where, and how he should best make use of his authority? It is not because Dr. Oxenham thinks that S. Peter, or his immediate successors, should have peremptorily issued dogmatic decrees on every conceivable occasion that anybody can reasonably conclude that the supremacy and infallibility are to be denied. On the lines of Dr. Oxenham's reasoning we might argue that the authority and prerogatives of any sovereign or ruler were to be rejected, simply because in a given number of instances that sovereign or ruler did not think fit to assert his prerogatives or to imperiously impose his legitimate authority upon his subjects. Our Lord Himself did not use His authority in that way. But Dr. Oxenham has strange ideas of what is meant by the supremacy of the Roman Pontiff, and of the manner in which it should be exercised.

As a matter of fact, there was no need for the Roman Bishops to pronounce personally, by dogmatic decrees, upon the almost innumerable heresies of the early centuries. The Church at large knew perfectly well, as her enemies did, that those errors struck at the very root of Christianity. That was obvious enough. These errors stood condemned by the elementary teaching of the Gospel. The Fathers and leaders of Christian thought were naturally at one upon such matters, and they had but to proclaim the fundamental principles of the Incarnation and Redemption to establish the truth in the minds of those who were willing to listen. And again, Dr. Oxenham forgets that during the three first centuries of the Church the Roman Pontiffs were constantly suffering persecution, often flying before their persecutors, hiding in the Catacombs, taking refuge in different directions, or dying at the stake in the amphitheatres. Those were not times when it was easy for them to be properly informed of the exact condition of things, and to be in a position to judge of the necessity of their personal intervention between conflicting parties, or of the possibility and wisdom of issuing dogmatic definitions and enactments of supreme authority.

But, is it a fact that the successors of S. Peter were silent for thirteen centuries, or for four hundred years, as Dr. Oxenham declares that they were, and that during all that period they did not exercise their supreme authority? Is it true that their supremacy was not acknowledged throughout those centuries? How does Dr. Oxenham get over the fact of S. Clement's intervention in Corinth, in the first century, or of Dionysius, Bishop of Alexandria, in the third century,—whose orthodoxy had been questioned,—directing his apology to Pope Dionysius, and receiving from him a comforting approval? How does he explain that eighty Bishops of Egypt should have written to Pope Liberius, in the middle of the fourth century, beseeching him to take up the cause of S. Athanasius, and that in their turn the Arian heretics should have called upon the Pope to use his authority

# TRADITION 87

against Athanasius?[1] In that same fourth century we find S. Basil appealing to Pope Damasus, and begging him to exercise his authority to provide for the needs of the Eastern Churches. And yet Dr. Oxenham asserts that "from the day when the Bishop of Rome began to claim supreme dominion, that claim was denied and rejected by the Eastern Churches as a novelty, uncatholic and unscriptural."[2]

Even the unbelieving Harnack, after stating that Chrysostom "is absolutely silent on the point" of peculiar prerogatives being assigned to the Bishop of Rome, goes on to say that the testimonies to a special dignity being possessed by the Roman Bishops are not wanting in the fourth century. And, strangely enough, he refers us to S. Chrysostom in his epistle to Pope Innocent I., and writes that "from A.D 380 this dignity bulked more largely in the eyes of Orientals." And then, though Harnack says that it was "without receiving a definite and fixed meaning," he adds: "Very characteristic in this respect are the Church Histories of Socrates and Sozomen, who on this point are free from partiality, and reflect *the universal opinion.* But it does not occur to them to doubt that the Roman Bishops had a *special authority and a unique relation to the whole Church.*" And, again, he makes the following important admissions: "There can be no doubt that even in the eyes of the Orientals there attached to the Roman

---

[1] Constant Ep. Rom. Pont., pages 272-279.   [2] Page 74.

Bishop a special something which was wanting to all the rest, a nimbus which conferred upon him a peculiar authority."[1] A very remarkable "nimbus" that bestowed so much! And did not S. Ambrose live in the fourth century? He it was who wrote that "Where Peter is, there is the Church."[2] The true Church, therefore, according to that great Saint and Father, cannot be found there where the successor of Peter is not. Nor did S. Ambrose think, with Dr. Oxenham, that Peter's successor was silent. It is recorded that Pope Siricius wrote to S. Ambrose, giving orders that Jovinian and his heretical disciples should be excommunicated, and S. Ambrose replies: "We have recognised in the letter of Your Holiness the watchfulness of the good shepherd, who dost faithfully guard the gate entrusted to thee, and with pious solicitude dost defend the fold of Christ."[3] And what has Dr. Oxenham to say of the testimony of S. Damasus, a Saint and a Pope of the fourth century, who writes as follows: "Although, dearest brethren, the decrees of the Fathers are known to you, yet we cannot wonder at your carefulness as regards the institutes of our forefathers that you cease not, *as the custom ever has been*, to refer all those things which can admit of any doubt to us as to the head that thence you may derive answers, whence you received the institution and rule of living rightly"?[4] And

---

[1] Hist. of Dogma, vol. iii. page 226.  [2] In Ps. xl.
[3] Migne P.L. 16.  [4] Ep. v. Prosp. Numid.

how does Dr. Oxenham reconcile his assertion with the letter of the great S. Jerome, addressed to Pope Damasus, in that same fourth century, in which he says:—"Envy, avaunt; away with the pride of the topmost dignity of Rome; I speak with the fisherman's successor, and the disciple of the cross. Following no chief but Christ, I am joined in communion with Your Holiness, that is with the chair of Peter. Upon that rock I know that the Church was built. Whosoever eats the lamb out of this house is profane. If any be not in the ark of Noah, he will perish whilst the deluge prevaileth. . . . Whosoever gathereth not with thee, scattereth, that is, whosoever is not of Christ, is anti-Christ"?[1] Let Dr. Oxenham consider these words of the Saints and Fathers of the fourth century, together with other similar texts in our Appendix. Would he be prepared to write to Leo XIII. to-day in such terms as those used by S. Ambrose and S. Jerome, and by so many others? If not, it remains for the reader to choose between the teaching of the Fathers and the theories put forward by Dr. Oxenham. He mentions S. Augustine, but S. Augustine, together with the Bishops of the Council of Milevis, at the beginning of the fifth century, wrote to Pope Innocent I.—"We think that those who hold such perverse and pernicious opinions will more readily yield to the authority of Your Holiness,

---

[1] Ep. xv., Damas Pap.

derived as it is from the authority of the Holy Scriptures."[1]

A merely negative argument, such as Dr. Oxenham would have us adopt, when he states that the prerogatives of the Bishop of Rome are not mentioned in the writings of certain Fathers in a given instance, without proving why those Fathers should necessarily have alluded to those prerogatives in that particular instance, is of absolutely no avail to establish the *absolute* silence, which, as we have shown from many other sources, cannot possibly be admitted. Dr. Oxenham would have had S. Augustine, in his controversy with the Donatists, use no other argument to convince them of their schism, but merely tell them that the Bishop of Rome was supreme and infallible; and Dr. Oxenham does not hesitate to assert that had S. Augustine "been acquainted with this one conclusive argument," he "might have saved himself the labour of writing seventy-five chapters, urging all sorts of other arguments; they were all mere waste of time and trouble."[2] As a matter of fact, S. Augustine, throughout his controversy with the Donatists, did appeal to the judgment of Pope Melchiades, and he calls it "the judgment of the Roman Bishop Melchiades, by which Caecilianus was purged and absolved."[3] Because Melchiades had said — "I decide that he (Caecilianus)

---

[1] Ep. 176, Migne P.L.    [2] Page 71.
[3] Ad Donat. post Collat. lib. unus.

should deservedly be kept in his ecclesiastical communion, his status being unimpaired."[1]   And S. Augustine calls it "a final sentence issued by the blessed Melchiades."[2]   Moreover, he tells the Donatists that Constantine committed the question to be discussed and terminated by bishops, "which also was done in the city of Rome under the presidency of Melchiades, the Bishop of that Church, with many of his colleagues."  Hence, though the judgment was a joint sentence, it is described by S. Augustine as the judgment of Melchiades.   Had the mere assertion of Papal claims sufficed as a conclusive argument in the eyes of the Donatists, no doubt S. Augustine would have gone no further, nor would the Donatists, nor any other heretics and schismatics, have ever rebelled against the Church, if such a simple proceeding had been enough to convince them of their error and bring them to submission.  No wonder that Protestants who, like Dr. Oxenham, have such a mistaken conception of the Pope's supremacy and infallibility, and the manner in which such prerogatives are exercised, no wonder, I say, that they should imagine that Catholics cannot think, nor reason, nor argue upon any point of religious controversy, simply because they believe in the special authority and infallible teaching of the See of Peter.

As to the historical parallel, of which Dr. Oxen-

---

[1] Optat. c. Parmen, lib. 1.    [2] Ep. 43, al. 162.

ham speaks on page 73 of his book, a parallel between Imperial and Christian Rome, it is based upon an assumption which he has yet to prove, and in the light of the Scriptural texts, and of the testimony of the Fathers, we cannot take it seriously. The learned writer, Dr. Salmon, whose opinions appear to be all but infallible in Dr. Oxenham's eyes, asserts a great deal, but he proves little or nothing in the aforesaid parallel. Undoubtedly, we may see in the fact of S. Peter's Chair having been established in Rome, the imperial city, and the great centre of the political world, a very remarkable disposition of Providence, and one which further enhances the dignity of the Apostolic See. But to conclude that the authority of that See owes its origin to the imperial dignity of the centre of civil power, is to ignore the evidence of Holy Scripture, and the teaching of the Fathers, and to beg the whole question. *Post hoc, ergo propter hoc* is a time-worn fallacy, and because two events follow one upon another in the order of time, or are in some way connected, that does not justify the conclusion that one is the origin and cause of the other, especially when there is so much evidence to prove that they were derived from totally different sources. One might as well argue that Christianity owes its origin to paganism, because our obelisks, with the Cross above them, have now become Christian monuments.

# S. VICTOR

(II.)

### S. Victor and the Eastern Churches

The short account given us by Dr. Oxenham of the main facts concerning the disputes which arose at the end of the second century between the Pope, S. Victor, and some of the Eastern Bishops (for they were only in a minority) is fairly accurate, though he misrepresents several of the circumstances, and fails to see that he is admitting that, after all, there was not the great silence on the part of the Roman Bishops, of which he spoke in the preceding pages. The disagreement as to the proper time for celebrating the Easter Festival, reached an acute stage in the time of S. Victor, and Eusebius, whom Dr. Oxenham quotes, does not tell us that S. Victor actually went the length of finally excommunicating those who did not conform to the prevailing custom, but that "he made the endeavour" (πειρᾶται.) We have not S. Victor's words, and therefore we cannot possibly say when the announcement of his intention was actually to come into force. And we need hardly remark that the subject of contention was not one of faith or of morals, but one of discipline. Some of the Eastern Bishops addressed an entreaty to Pope Victor, "exhorting him," as Eusebius says, and Polycrates, the Bishop of Ephesus, and others did so with considerable bitterness. Why be so concerned at S. Victor's attitude, and only exhort *him*, instead of addressing other Bishops, were it not that what he said and did was of such supreme importance? There is no truth in Dr. Oxenham's statement to the effect that S. Irenaeus reproved Victor "for assuming authority over the Easterns to which he had no right."[1] S. Irenaeus, as we shall see later on, teaches most emphatically that the authority of the See of Rome extends over all other Churches, as even Renan admits. In the case before us, he acted as mediator. He pointed out to S. Victor the evil results which were likely to ensue if the threats were carried out, and he feared that a schism might be the consequence of S. Victor's excessive severity. He recommended a milder course, and respectfully advocated that "whole churches should not be cut off." Hence he fully acknowledged S. Victor's authority, and he never suggested a doubt as to his right of exercising it over the Easterns, but he begged him not to use it in such a way; and the fact that S. Irenaeus and other Bishops were so anxious that the Pope should not make use of his supreme authority in that severe manner, points clearly to the acknowledged existence of Papal prerogatives. S. Victor acted in conformity with this advice, and the final result, as Dr. Oxenham is aware, was that the Eastern Churches accepted the Roman and universal observance. Had some of the Eastern communities not done so, and

---

[1] Page 77.

# S. CYPRIAN

if S. Victor had actually cut them off, they would have placed themselves in schism against his legitimate authority, wisely or unwisely exercised, as the case may be. But even in that hypothesis, nothing could be proved against their recognition of the supremacy or infallibility of the Bishops of Rome.

(III.)

### S. Stephen and S. Cyprian

It would be impossible, within the limit of these pages, to deal fully with the well-known disagreement between S. Cyprian and Pope Stephen in regard to the custom, upheld by S. Cyprian, of rebaptising those who had been baptised by heretics. The subject would indeed demand a special essay to discuss it thoroughly. Dr. Oxenham raises this great historical question in order to use it against Papal claims, but he finds it possible to discuss it in two pages of his little book, and then to draw far-reaching conclusions. We cannot follow his method of thus taking an unfair advantage of our readers. We would therefore urge them, if they wish to become acquainted with the sequence of events of that intricate period, and its available evidence, to refer to the standard works that have been published on the subject.[1] For the purpose of our present

---

[1] See for instance, The Hist. of the Church, by Hergenrœther, n. 193; The Primitive Church and the See of Rome, by Luke Rivington, pages 47-116.

argument, it will be sufficient to point out that S. Cyprian, like the other Fathers of the Church, certainly taught the supremacy and prerogatives of S. Peter and of his successors, and that he acted in accordance with that belief, notwithstanding his angry words at the time of his disagreement with Pope Stephen, not long before both he and that Pontiff won the martyr's crown.

And first as to his teaching. In two letters which he addressed to Pope Cornelius, S. Cyprian writes that the Roman Church " is the root and mother of the Catholic Church, the Chair of Peter and the principal Church, whence sacerdotal unity has its source."[1] In another epistle to the same Pope, he says:—" To be in communion with Cornelius (Pope) is to be in communion with the Catholic Church."[2] And again, in his celebrated treatise on the Unity of the Church, S. Cyprian declares:—The following is a short and easy proof of the faith. The Lord said to Peter, I say to thee thou art Peter; upon one alone He buildeth His Church; and *although* after His Resurrection He gives a similar power to all the Apostles, and says:—As the Father hath sent Me, etc., *nevertheless*, in order to make unity clear, by His own authority He laid down the source of that unity as beginning from one. Certainly, the other Apostles also were what Peter was, endowed with an equal fellowship both of honour and of

---

[1] Ep. 48 and 49, ad Corn.     [2] Ep. 55.

## S. CYPRIAN

power, *but* the commencement proceeds from unity, that the Church of Christ may be set forth as one."[1] Other similar texts may be quoted from the writings of S. Cyprian, but what he says in this treatise is all the more significant since he is dealing with the subject of the unity of the Church from a special point of view, and in order to show forth more particularly the rights of the bishops over the laity, and the necessity of union between each flock and its own pastor, so that his line of argument did not lead him to dwell at length upon the prerogatives of the mother-Church. And yet he speaks so distinctly, and he explains on the same principle as we have done in these pages, the relationship of the Apostles to S. Peter, their Prince and Head. In conformity with this teaching, S. Cyprian mentions Cornelius Bishop of Rome being appointed "when the place of Peter, and the rank of the sacerdotal chair was vacant." Dr. Oxenham will not find S. Cyprian using such expressions in connection with any other Bishop, or any other see, throughout the world.

Next, as to S. Cyprian's manner of acting. See how even when the "place of Peter" was vacant, after the death of Fabian, S. Cyprian far from resenting a letter addressed to him by the Roman clergy, who were not satisfied with the reports that had reached them of S. Cyprian's line of conduct, writes

---

[1] De Unit. n. 4.

to them in reply: "I have thought it necessary to write this letter to you, wherein an account might be given to you of my acts, discipline, and diligence."[1] Why did S. Cyprian submit his case to Rome, even when the see was vacant, if not because he turned naturally to Rome as the centre of authority, and because he thought, as he himself said, that the Romans are "they to whom faithlessness can have no access"?[2] Then again S. Cyprian appeals to Rome against a band of schismatics who had ventured to go there to urge their case, they themselves, too, giving testimony in this way to the supremacy of that see, and he writes: "Having had a pseudo-bishop ordained for them by heretics, they dare to set sail and to carry letters from schismatic and profane persons to the chair of Peter and the principal Church, whence the unity of the priesthood has taken its rise."[3] He appeals once more to the Pope in order that the latter should excommunicate Marcian, Bishop of Arles, because he had joined Novatian, urging the Pontiff to write "letters of plenary authority." And let the reader take note, the Pope was S. Stephen, the same Pontiff with whom S. Cyprian had his disagreement, and in that very disagreement, S. Cyprian appeals to the judgment of the Roman Pontiff by sending him the acts of his Council, much as that judgment displeased him when it was uttered. So that when Dr.

---

[1] Ep. 20.  [2] Ep. 59.  [3] *Ib.*

# S. CYPRIAN

Oxenham declares that "S. Cyprian and all the African Bishops declined to admit the authority claimed by S. Stephen," he goes far beyond the mark.

Strangely enough, Dr. Oxenham also informs us that, "Whether S. Cyprian was right as to the particular point in dispute between himself and the Pope is quite immaterial."[1] Yet, one would have thought that in argument against the supremacy and infallibility of the Pope, the question of who was right in the controversy was of paramount importance. And S. Stephen was right, as Dr. Oxenham well knows. S. Vincent of Lerins, whose authority even Anglicans are ready to admit, speaks of S. Stephen as "a holy and prudent man," and referring to the famous dispute, he says: "When therefore they all from every side cried out against the novelty of the thing, and all the bishops all around began to resist it, each according to his own zeal, then Pope Stephen, Prelate of the Apostolic See, together with his colleagues, but beyond the rest, withstood, thinking, as I presume, that it would be proper if he excelled all the rest in devotion of faith, as much as he surpassed them in authority of place. What then was the upshot of the whole business? What but the usual and customary issue. Antiquity was retained, novelty exploded."[2] And it was the Pope who guarded the traditional

---

[1] Page 79.   [2] Comm. 9.

**100**  PAPAL CLAIMS

teaching of antiquity, even against such an eminent man as S. Cyprian.

The Council of which Dr. Oxenham speaks on page 79 of his book took place in September, 256 A.D. Pope Stephen died in 257 A.D., and S. Cyprian the following year, both of them martyrs. The whole discussion came to an end in the time of S. Augustine, and Pope Stephen's reply to S. Cyprian remained as the law of the Universal Church. S. Augustine assures us that "peace was preserved in all essentials" between S. Stephen and S. Cyprian, and that the latter did not separate himself from the Pope because he was not a "son of perdition."[1] S. Augustine sums up his judgment of the whole case in opposition to Dr. Oxenham, and suggests that either the Donatists forged the documents, as they were wont to do, and that S. Cyprian did not say what is attributed to him, or that S. Cyprian, like the other Bishops, corrected his mistake, or, again, that his great perseverance in clinging to the unity of the Church covered the blot. "Moreover," writes S. Augustine, "there is this, that, as a most fruitful bough, the Father purged away whatever there was in him to be blotted out, by the sickle of his martyrdom."[2]

What conclusion, then, can be drawn from all this which in any way destroys the doctrine of the supremacy and infallibility of Peter's successors? The Church was founded upon the Rock, not upon

---

[1] Lib. De Bapt. 1-18.   [2] Ep. 93 ad Vincent.

# S. IRENAEUS 101

S. Cyprian, as he himself had taught, and if S. Cyprian, after acting wrongly, had separated himself from the centre of unity, S. Cyprian would have gone, and he would have lost the glory which is his; but the Church of Christ, with Peter as its foundation, would have remained, as it remains to-day.

(IV.)

## The Text of S. Irenaeus

1. We give elsewhere the translation of the whole text of S. Irenaeus, with the passages that precede and follow the portion quoted in Latin[1] by Dr. Oxenham (p. 83). It will be sufficient here to give that part of it with which we are chiefly concerned. S. Irenaeus writes as follows:—" But as it would be a very long task to enumerate, in such a volume as this, the successions of all the Churches; pointing out that tradition which the greatest and most ancient, and universally known, Church of Rome—

---

[1] "Traditionem itaque Apostolorum in toto mundo manifestam, in omni Ecclesia adest respicere omnibus qui vera velint videre: et habemus annumerare eos qui ab Apostolis instituti sunt Episcopi in Ecclesiis, et successores eorum usque ad nos, qui nihil tale docuerunt, neque cognoverunt quale ab his deliratur. Etenim si recondita mysteria scissent Apostoli, quae seorsum et latenter ab reliquis perfectos docebant, his vel maxime traderent ea quibus etiam ipsas Ecclesias committebant. Valde enim perfectos et irreprehensibiles in omnibus eos volebant esse, quos et successores relinquebant, suum ipsorum locum magisterii tradentes: quibus emendate egentibus fieret magna utilitas, lapsis autem summa calamitas. Sed quoniam valde longum est in hoc tale volumine omnium Ecclesiarum

founded by the two most glorious Apostles Peter and Paul—derives from the Apostles, and that faith announced to all men, which through the succession of (her) bishops has come down to us, we confound all those who in any way, whether through self-complacency or vain-glory, or blindness and perverse opinions, assemble otherwise than as behoveth them. FOR TO THIS CHURCH, ON ACCOUNT OF MORE POTENT PRINCIPALITY [OR PRE-EMINENT AUTHORITY], IT IS NECESSARY THAT EVERY CHURCH, THAT IS, THOSE WHO ARE ON EVERY SIDE FAITHFUL, RESORT [SHOULD BE IN CONCORD], IN WHICH (CHURCH) EVER, BY THOSE WHO ARE ON EVERY SIDE, HAS BEEN PRESERVED THAT TRADITION WHICH IS FROM APOSTLES." Thus writes S. Irenaeus in the second century, and this famous text is constantly quoted, either in its entirety or in part, as bearing testimony to the supremacy and infallibility of the See of Rome.

Commenting upon it, however, Dr. Oxenham asserts " that it is very doubtful whether he (Irenaeus) said anything at all about the authority of the Church

---

enumerare successiones, maximae, et antiquissimæ, et omnibus cognitae, a gloriosissimis duobus Apostolis Petro et Paulo Romae fundatae et constitutae Ecclesiae, eam quam habet ab Apostolis traditionem, et annuntiatam hominibus fidem, per successiones Episcoporum pervenientem usque ad nos indicantes, confundimus omnes eos, qui quoquo modo, vel per sibi placentia, vel vanam gloriam, vel per caecitatem et malam sententiam, praeterquam oportet colligunt. Ad hanc enim Ecclesiam propter potiorem [*or*, potentiorem] principalitatem necesse est omnem convenire Ecclesiam, hoc est, eos qui sunt undique fideles, in qua semper ab his, qui sunt undique, conservata est ea quæ ab Apostolis traditio." S. Irenaeus, Contra Hœreses, liber iii., cap. iii., §§ 1 and 2. Ed. Benedict. Paris, 1710.

# S. IRENAEUS  103

of Rome—his words seem most probably to refer to the City of Rome, not to the Church"; [1] Dr. Oxenham does not add a word to prove his statement that when Irenaeus said "Church" he most probably meant "City." We have seen that Renan himself did not venture upon such a misrepresentation of the text, and we may dismiss the matter by just reminding Dr. Oxenham that Mr. Puller, whose authority he so often quotes, in spite of all that he had written on the point, is now compelled to give up the interpretation to which Dr. Oxenham so fondly clings.

2. Leo XIII., in his Encyclical, quotes a portion of the last sentence of the text of S. Irenaeus, and in the authorised English translation it is given thus: "With this Church, on account of its pre-eminent authority, it is necessary that every Church should be in concord."[2] Dr. Oxenham objects to the expression "should be in concord," and prefers the reading "to resort to." In support of this translation of the words *convenire ad*, he refers us to the Latin edition of the Bible, which is irrelevant, for we are not discussing terms used in Scripture, nor are we dealing with the classics. Consequently, we must translate the words in keeping with the context; and, considering that S. Irenaeus is speaking of the "necessity" of every Church resorting to Rome in order to preserve the "faith and tradition of the Apostles," surely the

---

[1] Page 82.   [2] Satis cog. page 43.

translation, "should be in concord," is perfectly legitimate. But since Dr. Oxenham prefers the expression, "to resort to," let us accept it. The difference in the present instance is of minor consequence, for the argument remains the same. What does Dr. Oxenham imagine that S. Irenaeus meant by "resorting to Rome"? He could not intend that every Church throughout the world was to resort to Rome as the centre of trade or as a seat of political government and civil power, for he speaks of the necessity of every Church doing so in order to preserve the faith and tradition of the Apostles, and the reason that he gives is, "because of the more potent (or pre-eminent) authority" of the See of Rome. We are no nearer Dr. Oxenham's conclusion, even if we accept the different translation of "convenire ad," or if we substitute "principality" for "authority." His own comment seems to imply this, for on page 85 of his book he writes: "The witness to the true faith, which may be found in the Church of Rome as a prominent sample of an Apostolic Church, will, S. Irenaeus thinks, confound and confute all those who have gone astray after new and unauthorised doctrines." Yes, but according to S. Irenaeus the Church of Rome is not only *a prominent sample* of *an* Apostolic Church, but *the most prominent sample* of *the pre-eminently* Apostolic Church to which " it is necessary" that the faithful on every side should resort on account of more potent principality or

## S. IRENAEUS 105

authority. Dr. Oxenham adds that "the importance of the witness borne by the Church of Rome is not stated to consist in the supreme authority of the Bishop of Rome."[1] But has he forgotten that the Holy Spirit has entrusted to the Bishops the task of teaching and of guarding the true faith, and that the Bishop is in the Church and the Church in the Bishop? Moreover, the text distinctly tells us that the faith of Rome was "announced to all men, which through the succession of (her) Bishops has come down to us," and S. Irenaeus proceeds at once to give us the list of the Bishops of Rome from the time of the Apostles, mentioning them by name and in order of time. How can Dr. Oxenham presume to state that "Irenaeus, indeed, says nothing about the Bishop of Rome; he speaks of 'the Church'; but it consists, he says, in the fact that the Roman Church was one of those Churches, and there were several, which had an unbroken succession of Bishops and an unbroken tradition of faith."[2] Now, a glance at the text will show that Irenaeus places the Roman Church, and therefore the Bishop of that Church, on a totally different footing to all other Churches, and that Dr. Oxenham is simply misrepresenting S. Irenaeus, who did not speak of the Church of Rome as merely "one" of many equal Churches. And yet Dr. Oxenham hurls at Pope Leo XIII. the accusation of having "deliberately falsified the testimony of S. Irenaeus."[3]

---

[1] Page 85.     [2] Page 85.     [3] Pages 82-85.

# 106 PAPAL CLAIMS

3. After thus wantonly insulting the venerable Pontiff, Dr. Oxenham sets us several questions to answer. The task is a very simple one, and we will take the points as they are given. (1) "Why tell the heretics that they might appeal to any one of the several 'Apostolic Churches' which had the succession and tradition of faith, if the Church of Rome was the only one which had conclusive authority?"—Because, besides the Church to which it was "necessary" that every Church throughout the world should resort, according to S. Irenaeus, on account of her pre-eminent position and authority, there were other Churches, which had not that position, but whose orthodoxy and tradition were as yet unsullied by error. And such Churches might be appealed to, according to S. Irenaeus, as an additional argument. (2) "Why insist, as Irenaeus does, that it was the unbroken succession of their Bishops, and the unbroken tradition of their faith, which guaranteed the teaching of all these Apostolic Churches? Why give this misleading reason if the one true and sufficient reason was the assured infallibility of the Bishop of Rome?"—Because it was not misleading at all, but another argument in behalf of the same teaching, and perfectly consistent with what S. Irenaeus had said before, precisely because those other Churches were in communion with the "more potent" See of Rome, and testified to the same truth. (3) "Why go on, as S. Irenaeus does in the paragraph follow-

ing the one which we are considering, to appeal to the Church of Smyrna, to enumerate the Bishops of that Church, and call attention to the importance of its tradition as coming down from the Apostle S. John?"[1]—For the same reason, namely, to show forth, as further proof, the uniformity of the Apostolic faith and tradition, which all the Apostles taught, and which, *as a matter of fact*, was still preserved in those important Churches; just on the same principle as Leo XIII. reminds us of the faith and tradition of Catholic England before the Reformation, whilst asserting at the same time the supremacy and infallibility of the See of Rome. Nor is it true that in that paragraph S. Irenaeus enumerates the Bishops of Smyrna, though undoubtedly he could do so. Polycarp alone is mentioned by him, whereas the Bishops of Rome are fully enumerated. Apparently Dr. Oxenham does not allow S. Irenaeus to put forward several arguments in support of his teaching, if he gives one that is conclusive. This strange theory would be fatal to the writings of any author upon any subject. Dr. Oxenham himself gives us arguments in his book, which he describes as *conclusive*, and yet he does not hesitate to suggest many others.

4. We cannot conclude this paragraph without a word upon what we might call the climax of Dr. Oxenham's venture. He does nothing less than

---

[1] Page 87.

accuse Leo XIII. of mistranslating and suppressing the text of S. Irenaeus. And these are his words:— " Accordingly, some Roman writers, and we regret to find the present Pope among the number, quote the first half of the sentence, translating it so as to suit their purpose, and suppress the other half. Most remarkable, says the Pope, is the testimony of S. Irenaeus, who, referring to the Roman Church, says: 'With this Church, on account of its pre-eminent authority, it is necessary that every Church should be in concord,' and there the Pope stops, in the middle of the sentence, which goes on thus: 'in which Church the tradition, which comes down from the Apostles, is always preserved *by means of those who come thither from all parts.*"—A more daring attempt to travesty the truth could hardly be conceived. Dr. Oxenham gives us two translations of the text under consideration. Let us place them side by side.

| On page 84. | On page 89. |
|---|---|
| "To this Church (of Rome), because of its more influential principality, every Church, that is, the faithful from all parts, must resort, and in it the tradition which is from the Apostles is preserved *by those* who come from every quarter." | . . . . . "in which Church the tradition, which comes down from the Apostles, is always preserved *by means of* those who come thither from all parts." |

Dr. Oxenham interpolates the text in his second translation, and adds the expression " by means of," which does not appear in the first instance. After

# S. IRENAEUS

accomplishing this not very creditable performance, he tells us that the Pope "suppresses" the evidence. I refrain from qualifying such a proceeding, and I will only point out: (1) that the authentic text does not warrant the translation " by means of " as rendering the Latin words " ab his " in the context, and that, without in the slightest degree suppressing the evidence, the Pope could quote the first part of the sentence without the second if he so pleased; (2) that Dr. Oxenham's second translation introduces a contradiction which is inadmissible in the reasoning of S. Irenaeus. For it would imply that S. Irenaeus tells us, on the one hand, that the faithful from all parts must resort to Rome on account of her pre-eminent authority, or principality, in order that they might preserve the true faith and tradition of the Apostles; and, on the other hand, he would tell us that all the faithful are to maintain the true faith and tradition by means of *themselves*, and therefore *not* by resorting to the pre-eminent Church of Rome. How can such an interpretation be entertained for a moment? If, as Dr. Oxenham asserts, every Church was to resort to Rome, " so that what was taught in Rome was continually being tested by comparison with what was taught in other Churches,"[1] then, contrariwise, the Church of Rome would be resorting to other Churches, not those Churches to Rome: the more powerful principality, authority, pre-eminence, or

---

[1] Page 89.

even influence would cease to be, the "necessity" of resorting to Rome would not exist, and the whole meaning of the passage written by S. Irenaeus would vanish.

## PART V.

### COUNCILS OF THE CHURCH

A FEW remarks upon the Councils of the Church, their utility, and their connection with the prerogatives of the Roman Pontiff, will not be out of place here, and will enable us to point out the mistaken theories which are advanced by Dr. Oxenham at the end of his book. For he would have us believe that "if the Popes are, and always have been, what the Vatican Council asserts that they are, *then* all these great Church Councils, summoned to decide on questions of faith,—all of them, including the Vatican Council itself, were entirely needless, an enormous waste of time."[1] And Dr. Oxenham concludes that: "It is no exaggeration to say that the very existence of General Councils, called as they were, to decide disputes as to matters of faith, is of itself an open and evident contradiction of Papal claims, as they are now made. And that contradiction becomes more express and emphatic when we come to see what those Councils did when they had

---

[1] Page 92.

# COUNCILS 111

to deal with the position and claims of the Bishops of Rome."[1] Now, this manner of arguing is based once more upon the fallacy which has served Dr. Oxenham in good stead on previous occasions, and by which he makes it clear that he has a mistaken conception of the Catholic teaching regarding the supremacy and the infallibility of the Pope, and that he cannot distinguish between the existence of those prerogatives and the manner of using them in the government of the Church.

We may sum up the Catholic position in the following way:—(1) If the prerogatives of S. Peter and of his successors are established, as we hold that they are, by the teaching of Holy Scripture and of the Fathers, no Council can be truly Œcumenical, that is to say, a Council of the Universal Church, without the intervention and final sanction of the Head and Pastor of the whole Church, the rock upon which the Church is built; and the infallibility of a General Council is inadmissible without the formal approval of him to whom the care of the whole flock was solemnly committed by Christ Himself, because the Episcopate cannot be separated from its head. (2) General Councils are not an *absolute* and indispensable necessity for the teaching and government of the Church, under all circumstances, because S. Peter's office is ever there to safeguard the teaching, and to provide for the government of Christ's kingdom. Accord-

---

[1] Page 93.

ingly, the Church existed for three hundred years without a General Council, but it never existed without the Chair of Peter. On the other hand, as a practical means of attaining more fully a given object under special circumstances a General Council may be both necessary and useful. Hence, General Councils have ever been one of the chief means of teaching and of governing the Church, and when really Œcumenical, with the Supreme Pontiff as Head, they are necessarily infallible. (3) The Pope may be present at an Œcumenical Council, either in person, and then he pronounces his judgment, together with, and presiding over the other Bishops, who are judges in Council; or he may be present in the person of his legates. These legates, in their turn, may attend the Council with full instructions and full powers to express the judgment of the Pontiff, and to formulate decrees in his name, or, in matters which require debating, the legates may appear at the Council with limited powers, and with the obligation of referring the decrees issued there to the Roman Pontiff, for that final sanction of his which renders those decrees irrevocable,—absolutely so in matters of faith and morals, and relatively so in questions of discipline. (4) Whilst the Roman Pontiff possesses the fullest prerogatives of supremacy and infallibility, he is human, and must use them in relation to men and the conditions of mankind, and Councils are therefore most useful as a practical means of extirpating heresies throughout the world, of reforming abuses,

# NICAEA 113

of scattering national prejudices, and, by means of debate, of rendering the truth more manifest in the minds of the Bishops and of the faithful. Moreover, not only the faithful and persons well disposed, but heretics and schismatics too, are naturally more likely to be reached by an Œcumenical Council, and to be more unfailingly impressed by the solemnity of its action in union with the Pope. So much for Dr. Oxenham's " enormous waste of time and labour."

(I.)

### The Council of Nicaea (325 A.D.)

There is very little to object to in the paragraph which Dr. Oxenham gives us on the First General Council and its sixth canon, which decreed thus: " That the old custom shall hold good in Egypt, and Lybia, and Pentapolis, that is, that the Bishop of Alexandria has authority over all those provinces; for there is a similar custom with reference to the Bishop of Rome, and likewise in the case of Antioch, and the other provinces let the old rights be preserved."[1] The Pope presided at this Council by his Legates, Hosius, Bishop of Cordova, and two priests, Vito and Vincentius, and these three signed first, because they were Papal Legates, and before Alexandria, Antioch, and Jerusalem. Notice how the Coun-

---

[1] Hefele. History of Councils, vol. i., book ii., cap. ii., 42.

# 114 PAPAL CLAIMS

cil points to Rome as the model to take as regards the jurisdiction of a metropolitan see. Dr. Oxenham appears to lose sight of the fact that the Bishop of Rome is not only the successor of S. Peter, and Supreme Pontiff of the whole Church, but also the first Patriarch of the West, Primate of Italy, Archbishop and Metropolitan of the Roman province. Leo XIII. bears these titles to-day. Consequently, we can quite agree with Dr. Oxenham when he says: "It is plain from this canon (6th) that the Council of Nicaea recognised the Bishop of Rome as a metropolitan, having jurisdiction over all the province of Rome, just as the Bishops of Antioch, Alexandria, and the other metropolitans had jurisdiction each in his own particular province. Thus the Bishop of Rome was, in the eyes of the Council of Nicaea, Metropolitan in his own province." Where we cannot be at one with Dr. Oxenham is in the very last words of his paragraph, for he adds: "and he was nothing more."[1] That is precisely what we deny, on the grounds which we have already explained throughout these pages.

(II.)

### The Sardican Canon

Dr. Oxenham admits that the "Council of Sardica" was not an Œcumenical Council, and we need not stop to discuss how far the Sardican Canons consti-

---

[1] Page 95.

# SARDICA

tuted a separate Council, or were practically an appendix to the Council of Nicaea. Suffice it to say that the statement that "its canons were never received at all in the East"[1] is inaccurate, because these canons were received later on in the Eastern Churches, and were incorporated in their codes.[2] But what concerns us here is that the Sardican decree itself, far from proving Dr. Oxenham's point, proves just the contrary. He places the matter before us in the following way:—"But then arose the question, What should be done supposing some Bishop should complain that his own metropolitan, or his provincial synod, had not dealt justly with him? Was there to be no further appeal?"[3] And then Dr. Oxenham speaks of Hosius, Bishop of Cordova, in Spain, presiding over the Council, without mentioning that this prelate of a local and distant see presided because he was Papal Legate—that right therefore being already acknowledged as a matter of course, even in those early days. The Sardican Canon is then given us by Dr. Oxenham, in the form of a proposal by Hosius, quoted from Hefele's version, as follows:—"If it please you, let us honour the memory of the blessed Apostle Peter by allowing those who have looked into the case (*i.e.*, the case of any who complained of injustice) to write to Julius, Bishop of Rome; and if he thinks the case ought to be reconsidered, let him

---

[1] Page 95.
[2] The Prim. Ch. and the See of Rome, by L. Rivington, page 181.
[3] Page 96.

reopen the case and appoint judges."[1] Now, what does all this imply? It is simply the condemnation of the theory of national Churches. The ultimate appeal of a Bishop against his Metropolitan, and his own Provincial Synod, is to go to the Bishop of Rome. Why Rome, always Rome? Dr. Oxenham tells us that here "we have a great Council of Western Bishops allowing the Bishop of Rome to receive appeals from beyond his own province, as if it were something quite new, as indeed it was, and then directing him what he is to do if any appeal should be made to him."[2] This is absolutely contrary to the obvious evidence of the text, which speaks of honouring "the memory of the blessed Apostle Peter." It was anything but a new idea, and the appeal was to be made to Rome, therefore, because the Bishop of Rome was the successor of the blessed Apostle Peter. And, by the by, has Dr. Oxenham forgotten that he questioned the fact of S. Peter being Bishop of Rome? What does the Sardican canon tell him in connection with that point? Moreover, the decree says that the Pope is to decide whether the case is to be reopened or not, and that he, no one else, is to appoint the judges. And he is to be free to send a legate to discuss the case, either by himself, or with the other Bishops of the province in proximity with the one in which the case arose.[3] What could be more fatal to Dr. Oxen-

---

[1] Page 96. [2] Page 97.
[3] Diss. Hist. Eccl., vol. ii., Jungmann.

ham's conclusion? S. Athanasius, speaking of the Council of Tyre, and of the Bishops who had acted against him, writes thus: "both they and we were summoned."[1] They were summoned by Pope Julius, who is the Pontiff named in the very document before us. And S. Athanasius gives us a letter of that same Pope, who, with reference to the Bishops who upheld the decree of the Council of Tyre, writes thus: "Why was nothing said to us about the Church of Alexandria in particular? If, then, any suspicion rested upon the bishop there, notice thereof ought to have been sent to the Church of this place (Rome); whereas, after neglecting to inform us, and proceeding on their own authority as they pleased, now they desire to obtain our concurrence in their decisions. . . . Not so have the directions of the Fathers prescribed. This is another form of procedure, a novel practice. . . . What we have received from the blessed Apostle Peter, that I signify unto you."[2] How can Dr. Oxenham, in the face of such evidence, speak of the Sardican canon as a novelty, and say that it was "extending the jurisdiction of the Bishop of Rome and conferring on him a measure of authority which he had not before possessed"?[3] Pope Julius is able to point to antiquity and tells us that the "novelty" is to be found in the opposite course.

---

[1] Apol. con. Arian. 1.
[2] Athan. Hist. Tract., Lib. of Fathers, page 56.
[3] Page 97.

## 118   PAPAL CLAIMS

(III.)

### The Second General Council (381 A.D.)

There exists a so-called canon of the Second General Council, which is thus recited: "The Bishop of Constantinople shall hold the first rank next to the Bishop of Rome, because Constantinople is new Rome."[1] I describe it as a "so-called" canon, because S. Leo assures us that it was the work of only "certain Bishops," and Canon Bright, an Anglican authority, tells us that it gives an unfaithful representation of the facts, and that "it is certain that the Bishop of Rome enjoyed this pre-eminence not simply because this city was Rome, but also because he held the chair of Peter."[2] Dr. Oxenham presents this so-called canon to his readers as a Canon of the Council, but we do not possess documentary evidence of the discussions of the Council, and if this so-called canon was in any way brought forward at the Council, it could only be the proposal of a few of the 150 Fathers present, "certain bishops" as S. Leo tells us, and therefore not a Canon of the Council. A general Synod of Western Bishops refused to acknowledge it as a Canon of the Church, and the evidence, as far as it is available, shows that it was never appealed to in all the troubles between Theophilus and Chrysostom, nor

---

[1] Hefele. Hist. of Councils, vol. ii., book vii., page 98.
[2] Hist. of the Church, page 178.

is it mentioned as a Canon even in the earliest Greek records. And after all, Dr. Oxenham is a Western! He himself seems to feel uncertain about his own argument, for he remarks that "happily we are not obliged to rely on any inference, obvious or *doubtful*,"[1] and he hurries on to drop the matter and to discuss the Council of Chalcedon, where he feels more at home.

The chief points under consideration at the Council of Constantinople, were the maintenance of the Nicene creed, and the ordination of Flavian, and even Dr. Oxenham can only speak of the so-called canon as containing "a brief reference to the Bishop of Rome."[2] He should have reminded his readers that in that brief reference the question of the Pope's supremacy was not under consideration at all. The so-called canon deals with the subject of the Patriarchates in the East and West. The Popes had wished to reserve for the See of Rome the Patriarchate of the West, partly, no doubt, because Rome was the old capital of the Empire, without any detriment to their special prerogatives as occupants of the See of Peter and of his office over the Universal Church; prerogatives, which, as we have seen, did not rest upon any ecclesiastical organisation made by the Bishops of Rome or by any one else, but upon the Divine promises. The Bishop of Rome was, by his own will, Patriarch of the West, but he was a great deal more,

---

[1] Page 100.    [2] Page 99.

by the will of Christ. And therefore it was that the
Emperor Theodosius, at that same period of history,
did not hesitate to embody the general belief in his
decree: "We will that all people who are governed
by our clemency should practise the same religion as
the divine Apostle Peter delivered to the Romans, as
the religion proclaimed by him to this time declares
it; and which it is clear that the Pontiff Damasus
follows, and Peter, the Bishop of Alexandria, a man
of apostolic sanctity. . . . Those who follow this
law we order to take the name of Catholic Christians." As Father Rivington remarks, Theodosius,
the imperial neophyte, draws a distinction between
Damasus, whom he mentions as the Pontiff, and the
Bishop of Alexandria, whom he refers to as a man of
apostolic sanctity, and whose example of adherence
to the religion proclaimed by Peter should be followed in the East. Nor do we discover the slightest
indication of surprise in the East at the Emperor
pointing to Rome and the See of Peter, as the central
authority, and the seat of the Pontiff of the Christian
religion.[1] And that is sufficient for our present purpose.

(IV.)

### THE COUNCIL OF CHALCEDON

The much debated question of the 28th Canon,
which was passed by one-third of the Bishops who

---

[1] See the Prim. Ch. and the See of Peter, by L. Rivington, page 245.

# CHALCEDON

had sat in council at Chalcedon, and which many have endeavoured to foist upon us as a genuine Canon of that Œcumenical Council, is a question that has many ramifications, and we can only discuss it here, within the limits of Dr. Oxenham's line of argument. The text of that 28th Canon is given us by Hefele, and is as follows in Dr. Oxenham's book:—" As in all things we follow the ordinances of the holy Fathers, and as we know the recently-read canon of the 150 Bishops (of the Council of Constantinople), so do we decree the same in regard to the privileges of the most holy Church of Constantinople, which is new Rome. Rightly, therefore, have the Fathers bestowed upon the See of old Rome its privileges on account of its character as the imperial city; and moved by the same considerations the 150 Bishops awarded the like privileges to the most holy See of new Rome; judging, with good reason, that the city, which has the honour of being the seat of the Empire and of the Senate, and which enjoys equal (civil) privileges with old Rome, should also be honoured with equal ecclesiastical dignity, and should hold the second place next to that of old Rome."

Now, we must first notice that here, again, the document before us is not dealing directly with the special prerogatives of the supremacy and infallibility of Peter's successor, but with the question of the Patriarchal position of Rome and of Constantinople. We shall see presently how those who drew up this 28th Canon did themselves consider the See of Rome to be on a totally different footing to Constantinople and to be empowered with a supreme authority. This canon may be described as the result of a plot, on the part of certain Eastern Bishops, who, supported by the civil power, were intent upon obtaining for Constantinople a superiority over Alexandria and Antioch, in opposition to what had been settled at Nicaea. Accordingly, they appeal to the fact of Constantinople enjoying the same "civil" privileges with old Rome, and to her being the "seat of the Empire and of the Senate." This 28th Canon was not included in the programme of the Council of Chalcedon. Two-thirds of the Bishops had left, after concluding the real business of the Council, and the Papal Legates refused to attend this appendix to the Council, set on foot by a fraction of its members. Not one of the Western Bishops was present. And it was under these circumstances that the 28th Canon was drawn up. How can Dr. Oxenham present it to us as a genuine decree and canon of the Œcumenical Council of Chalcedon?

The Papal Legates proceeded to protest energetically against the novelty, inconsistent as it was with the Nicaean settlement. Their powers, as regards the Council proper, were at an end, but they followed the instructions which they had received from Pope Leo, and protested against a measure that had nothing to support it, save the ambition of civil and political rule. However, even the Imperial Commissioners declared that Rome had the ($\pi\rho\omega\tau\epsilon\hat{\iota}\alpha$) the primacy,

# CHALCEDON 123

and indeed it would have been idle to question this, nor did they think of doing so, but they urged that Constantinople should be granted in the East the honorary privileges (πρεσβεῖα) which old Rome possessed in the West, over and above the special prerogatives reserved to the See of Peter, and which no one could question or claim to equal. The Patriarchate of the East was what they were aiming at. We might add, perhaps, in regard to the 28th Canon itself, as it is worded, that if, when speaking of the patriarchal privileges, it be said that "the Fathers" bestowed them upon old Rome, first and foremost were the Bishops of Rome themselves, who thus claimed their right to assume patriarchal privileges, besides their divinely given prerogatives, and that the other Fathers can only be said to have "bestowed" them, inasmuch that they fully acknowledged them.

Dr. Oxenham admits that Pope Leo objected to the 28th Canon, when it was submitted to him. Pope Leo not only objected to it, he rejected it. And not until centuries afterwards did the Lateran Council (1215 A.D.) allow Constantinople the position which had been aspired to by *New Rome*, and only when Antioch and Alexandria had forfeited any reasonable claim to their former preponderance. But the 28th Canon was never accepted. In spite of the Pope's opposition, the decree was passed by those comparatively few Bishops, who had been sitting with the others at the Council of Chalcedon; and then what did this fraction proceed to do next? Dr. Oxenham does not tell his readers, but we shall do so. Those very Bishops appealed at once to Pope Leo, and used every possible endeavour to persuade him to sanction what they had accomplished. This appeal is, in itself, most significant. They wrote to the Pontiff that he was "the interpreter of the voice of Peter," that he was the "father of Constantinople," that "the vineyard had been entrusted to him by the Saviour"; they expressed the hope that as the "father of Constantinople" he would "extend his wonted care over that part of the vineyard," and they addressed him, saying: "Thou wast constituted the interpreter of the voice of blessed Peter to us all, and didst bring to all the blessing of his faith. Whence we also show the inheritance of truth to the children of the Church."[1] This, indeed, was according to the principle laid down by S. Irenaeus, in the second century, that every Church throughout the world should resort to the Church of Rome, in order to preserve the faith of the Apostles, on account of its pre-eminent principality and authority. Would the Anglican Bishops write in these terms to-day to Pope Leo XIII.? And, if not, what must be our conclusion? S. Leo would not give way, and Dr. Oxenham tells us that "his reason for objecting is that this decree (28th Canon) violates the ordinances of the great Council of Nicaea," which, he says, were enacted "under the

---

[1] Leo. Ep. 98, § 1.

# CHALCEDON 125

teaching of the Holy Spirit," and ought not to be altered."[1] Quite so. Does not this remind us of the words of the decree enacted by the Apostles at Jerusalem: "It has seemed good to the Holy Ghost and to us"? S. Leo uses the most powerful argument that he could use, for the great Council of Nicaea, approved by the Pope, who had presided over it by his Legates, was the first Œcumenical Council, after the Council of Jerusalem. And yet, because S. Leo does not merely reply by asserting the prerogatives of the See of Rome, Dr. Oxenham would have us accept his conclusion that even Pope Leo, "great champion as he was of Papal rights, even he did not hold and believe that theory of Papal supremacy."[2] The Bishops who had thus appealed to Rome and failed to obtain the Pontiff's sanction for their 28th Canon, remained recalcitrant in regard to it, supported as they were by the ambition of civil authority. But what of that? Does Dr. Oxenham hold that an act of insubordination is sufficient to justify us in denying the existence of a legitimate authority, or that it always and necessarily implies that those who disobey absolutely reject that authority, especially when they appeal to it and assert it, as those very Bishops did?—To conclude, the 28th Canon was rejected by the Pope, and as the Pope's sanction is essential in order to constitute an Œcumenical decree, because his preroga-

---

[1] Page 104.  [2] Page 106.

tives of universal Shepherd and Rock of the Church rest upon the Divine promise contained in Holy Scripture, it is idle to pretend that the 28th Canon was a decree of the Œcumenical Council of Chalcedon.

### Conclusion

There was a time when "Merry England" never doubted the prerogatives of S. Peter and of his successors, the Bishops of Rome. For a thousand years, her clergy and her laity, her Sovereigns and their people, loved to abide in communion with the Rock upon which the Church was built, and to cling to the guidance and rule of the Chief Shepherd. Those were the days of Augustine, of Lancfranc, of Anselm and of Theobald, of Fisher, and of More. The memories of those days still hover round the great Cathedrals of England, and linger in her Universities and Colleges, and in the most important institutions of the realm. Nor can history be written without placing this on record. It was then that the great English Doctor, Venerable Bede (673-731 A.D.) voiced the universal belief, and wrote: "And therefore did Blessed Peter, having confessed Christ with a true faith and followed him with a true love, receive in a special manner the keys of the Kingdom of heaven and the sovereignty of judicial power, that all the faithful throughout the world might understand that whosoever separate themselves from the unity of faith or from his fellowship can neither be released from the chains of their sins nor enter the gate of the heavenly Kingdom."[1] It was then, too, that the Prelates of the Province of Canterbury (1318 A.D.) addressed the Pope in terms such as these: "We, though unworthy, being included in your pastoral charge, and ourselves derived, as rivers from the fountain-head, from the exalted throne of the Holy Apostolic See . . . cast ourselves at your feet, who hold the highest Apostolic office . . . your servants, and the servants of your Church of the Province of Canterbury, who are ever ready to obey your Apostolic behests. . . . Long may the Papal dignity, reverenced above all others, flourish under your governance of the Universal Church."[2] God grant that those days may return once again, and banish unbelief and doubt from the mind of the English people.

A "branch theory" has been devised as a compromise with which to satisfy the yearnings of many an aching heart. But, alas! without avail. We too hold a "branch theory," but the branch theory of which our Blessed Saviour spoke. Branches there are, and there must be, in the One Church, but not branches without a stem and cut off from the vine, with their leaves scattered "High" and "Low" and "Broad." Our Lord spoke of such branches, and said: "If any one abide not in Me, he shall be cast

---

[1] Hom. lib. 16.
[2] Baigent's Registers, pages xii.-xliv., 90-93.

forth as a branch, and shall wither."[1] The Church is the mystical Body of Christ, and where Peter is, there is the Church, as the Fathers said of old.

When Newman was studying the testimony of the Fathers in the hope of finding arguments in behalf of the Anglican position, he wrote: "It was difficult to make out how the Eutychians or Monophysites were heretics, unless Protestants and Anglicans were heretics also; difficult to find arguments against the Tridentine Fathers, which did not tell against the Fathers of Chalcedon; difficult to condemn the Popes of the sixteenth century without condemning the Popes of the fifth. The drama of religion, and the combat of truth and error, were ever the same. The principles and proceedings of the Church now were those of the Church then; the principles and proceedings of heretics then were those of Protestants now. I found it so—almost fearfully; there was an awful similitude, more awful, because so silent and unimpassioned, between the dead records of the past and the feverish chronicle of the present. The shadow of the fifth century was on the sixteenth. It was like a spirit rising from the troubled waters of the old world, with the shape and lineaments of the new. The Church then, as now, might be called peremptory and stern, resolute, over-bearing, and relentless; and heretics were shifting, changeable, reserved, and deceitful, ever courting the civil power,

---

[1] John xv. 6.

and never agreeing together, except by its aid; and the civil power was ever aiming at comprehensions, trying to put the invisible out of view, and substituting expediency for faith. What was the use of continuing the controversy or defending my position, if, after all, I was forging arguments for Arius or Eutyches, and turning devil's advocate against the much-enduring Athanasius and the majestic Leo? Be my soul with the Saints! and shall I lift up my hand against them? Sooner may my right hand forget her cunning, and wither out-right, as his who once stretched it out against the prophet of God! anathema to a whole tribe of Cranmers, Ridleys, Latimers, and Jewels! perish the names of Bramhall, Ussher, Taylor, Stillingfleet, and Barrow from the face of the earth, ere I should do ought but fall at their feet in love and in worship, whose image was continually before my mind, and whose musical words were ever in my ears and on my tongue."[1]

May Dr. Oxenham reach the same conclusion, as he reads the works of the Fathers, and let him rest assured that, if this grace is bestowed upon him, he will have no truer friend than the author of these pages.

---

[1] Apol. Part v., page 211.

# APPENDIX

## (A) The Vatican Council

"Wherefore, resting on plain testimonies of the Sacred Writings, and adhering to the plain and express decrees both of our predecessors the Roman Pontiffs, and of the General Councils, we renew the definition of the Œcumenical Council of Florence, in virtue of which all the faithful of Christ must believe that the Holy Apostolic See and the Roman Pontiff possesses the primacy over the whole world, and that the Roman Pontiff is the successor of Blessed Peter, Prince of the Apostles, and is true Vicar of Christ, and Head of the whole Church, and Father and Teacher of all Christians; and that full power was given to him in Blessed Peter to rule, feed, and govern the Universal Church by Jesus Christ our Lord, as is also contained in the acts of the General Councils and in the Sacred Canons. Hence we teach and declare that by the appointment of our Lord the Roman Church possesses a superiority of ordinary power over all other Churches, and that this power of jurisdiction of the Roman Pontiff, which is truly episcopal, is immediate. . . . But so far is this power of the Supreme Pontiff from being any prejudice to the ordinary and immediate power of episcopal jurisdiction, by which Bishops, who have been set by the Holy Ghost to succeed and hold the place of the Apostles, feed and govern, each his own flock, as true Pastors, that this their episcopal authority is really asserted, strengthened, and protected by the supreme and universal Pastor; in accordance with the words of S. Gregory the Great: 'My honour is the honour of the whole Church. My honour is the firm strength of my brethren. I am truly honoured when the honour due to each and all is not withheld.'" (Vat. Coun. chap. 3 on the Primacy.) . . . "And because the sentence of our Lord Jesus Christ cannot be passed by, Who said: Thou art Peter, and upon this Rock I will build My Church, these things which have been said are approved by events, because in the Apostolic See the Catholic Religion and her holy and well-known doctrine has always been kept undefiled. . . . For the Holy Spirit was not promised to the successors of Peter that by His revelation they might make known new doctrine, but that by His assistance they might inviolably keep and faithfully expound the revelation or deposit of faith delivered through the Apostles. And, indeed, all the venerable Fathers have embraced, and the holy orthodox Doctors have venerated and followed, their Apostolic doctrine, knowing most fully that this See of holy Peter remains ever free from all blemish of error, according to the divine promise of the Lord our Saviour, made to the Prince of His disciples: I have prayed for

… APPENDIX iii

thee that thy faith fail not, and when thou art converted confirm thy brethren. . . . Therefore, faithfully adhering to the tradition received from the beginning of the Christian faith for the glory of God our Saviour, the exaltation of the Catholic Religion and the salvation of Christian people, the Sacred Council approving, we teach and define that it is a dogma divinely revealed; that the Roman Pontiff, when he speaks 'ex cathedra,' that is, when in discharge of the office of Pastor and Doctor of all Christians, by virtue of his supreme Apostolic authority, he defines a doctrine regarding faith or morals to be held by the Universal Church, by the divine assistance promised to him in Blessed Peter, is possessed of that infallibility with which the divine Redeemer willed that His Church should be endowed for defining doctrine regarding faith or morals; and that therefore such definitions of the Roman Pontiff are irreformable of themselves, and not from the consent of the Church." (Vat. Coun. chap. 4 on the Infallibility.)

(*B*) S. Augustine's Retractations (Lib. 1 Cap. 21)

"When I was a priest I also wrote a book against the epistle of Donatus, who was the second Donatian bishop in Carthage after Majorinus, an epistle in which he claims that the baptism of Christ is to be believed to exist only in his communion. In that book of mine, speaking of the Apostle Peter, I said that upon him, as upon a rock (petra), the Church was founded; and this interpretation [of the text] is sung by many in the verses of the most blessed Ambrose, where he says: . . . But I know that I have since very often explained that what was said by the Lord: Thou art Peter, and on this rock I will build My Church, should be understood as, upon Him Whom Peter confessed, saying: Thou art Christ, the Son of the living God; and thus Peter, so named from the rock (petra), would represent the person of the Church which is built upon this rock, and received the keys of the kingdom of heaven. FOR IT WAS NOT SAID TO HIM, 'Thou art rock (petra),' but 'Thou art Peter (Petrus).' But the rock (petra) was Christ, Whom Simon confessed, as the whole Church confesses Him, and was called Peter (Petrus). But of these two opinions let the reader choose whichever he thinks more probable."

## (*C*) TEXT OF S. IRENAEUS

"Therefore, *in every Church* (in omni Ecclesia adest respicere) there is at hand for all those who would fain see the truth a means of recognising the tradition of the Apostles made manifest throughout the whole world; and we have it in our power to enumerate those who were by the Apostles instituted Bishops in the Churches, and the successors of those Bishops down to ourselves, none of whom either taught or knew anything like unto the wild opinions of these men [heretics]. For if the Apostles had known any hidden mysteries, which they apart and secretly taught the perfect only, they would have delivered those mysteries, before all others, to those to whom they even entrusted the very Churches. For they wished that they whom they left as successors, delivering unto them their own office as teachers, should be especially perfect and blameless in everything; whose upright conduct in the discharge of their office would be of great profit, as their fall would be the greatest calamity. But as it would be a very long task to enumerate in a volume such as this the successions of all the Churches, we confute all those who in any way, whether through self-complacency or vainglory, or blindness and perverse opinion, assemble otherwise than is right, by pointing to that tradition which the greatest and most ancient and universally known Church of Rome—founded and constituted by the two most glorious Apostles Peter and Paul—has from the Apostles, and by pointing to that faith [of hers] proclaimed to mankind, which through the succession of her bishops has come down to us. For to this Church (of Rome) it is necessary that every Church, that is, the faithful on every side, resort, on account of her more potent principality, in which Church (of Rome) the tradition which is from the Apostles is ever preserved by those in all parts. The blessed Apostles, therefore, having founded and built up that Church, committed to Linus the episcopal office for the government of that

Church. Paul makes mention of this Linus in his Epistles to Timothy. To him succeeded Anacletus, and after him, the third from the Apostles who obtained that episcopacy was Clement, who had seen and conferred with the Apostles themselves, and who had still before his eyes the recent preaching and the tradition of the Apostles. Nor was he the only one, for many were then alive who had been instructed by the Apostles. . . . But to this Clement succeeded Evaristus; and to Evaristus, Alexander; and next to him, the sixth from the Apostles, Sixtus was appointed; and after him Telesphorus, who suffered a glorious martyrdom; next Hyginus; then Pius; after whom came Anicetus. Soter succeeded Anicetus, and now, the twelfth in succession from the Apostles, Eleutherius holds the episcopate. By this order and by this succession that tradition which is in the Church from the Apostles, and the preaching of the truth, have come down to us. And this is a most complete demonstration that the life-giving faith is one and the same, which, from the time of the Apostles until to-day, has been maintained in the Church, and transmitted in truthfulness." (Adv. Haeres, lib. iii. c. 3.)


## (D) TESTIMONY OF THE EARLY FATHERS

### *Century I.*

S. CLEMENT OF ROME.—See page 29.

# APPENDIX vii

## Century II.

S. Irenaeus.—See Appendix p. iv.

Tertullian.—" Was anything hidden from Peter, who was called the Rock whereon the Church was to be built, who received the keys of the kingdom of heaven, and the power of loosing and of binding in heaven and on earth" (De Praes. Haer. n. 22). *When a Montanist, Tertullian fell into the error of denying that the "keys" were given to the Church through Peter, but whilst expounding his error he still affords us evidence of the general belief of the Church, by appealing to it as a basis for his argument.* "Who art thou, overthrowing and changing the Lord's manifest intention, which confers this on Peter personally? Upon *thee*, He says, I will build My Church; and I will give to *thee* the keys, not to the Church; and whatsoever *thou* shalt bind, or *thou* shalt loose, not what *they* shall bind, or *they* shall loose. . . . In him the Church was built up, that is to say, through him. He first placed the key in the lock." (De Pudicitia, 21.)

## Century III.

Origen.—"Peter was called a Rock by the Lord, for to him is said: Thou art Peter, and upon this rock I will build My Church" (Comm. in Matt. n. 139). "When the chief authority in relation to the feeding of the sheep was delivered to Peter, and the Church was founded on him, as on the earth," etc. (In Ep. ad Rom. tom. iv. lib. 5), " and the gates of hell shall not prevail against it—what is the *it?* Is it the rock upon which Christ builds the Church, or the Church? The expression, indeed, is ambiguous, as if the Rock and the Church were one and the same. I indeed think that this is so, and that neither against the Rock upon which Christ builds His Church, nor against the Church, shall the gates of hell prevail. . . . For the Church, as the edifice of Christ, who has wisely built His house upon a Rock, cannot be conquered by the gates of hell, which may prevail over any man who shall be off the Rock and outside the Church, but shall be powerless against it " (Comm. in Matt. tom. xii. 2). "But, as it was befitting, notwithstanding that something was said of Peter in common with those who should thrice admonish the brethren, that Peter should be endowed with something peculiar above those who should thrice admonish; this was previously laid down regarding Peter, thus: 'I will give to thee the keys of the kingdom of heaven,' before saying and 'whatsoever ye shall bind on earth,' etc. And, indeed, if we carefully consider the gospels, even there we may see, regarding those things which appear to be common to Peter and to those who have thrice admonished the brethren, much difference and pre-eminence in the words addressed to Peter beyond those spoken in the second instance" (Comm. in Matt. tom. xiii.

31). [*N.B.—It is quite true that Origen has sometimes interpreted the text in S. Matthew allegorically and extended its meaning without destroying the literal interpretation.* See Introductory, p. 4.]

S. CYPRIAN (See page 95).—"There is one Baptism, and one Holy Spirit, and one Church founded by Christ our Lord upon Peter, as the source and principle of unity" (Ep. 60, ad Januar.). "For to Peter, upon whom He built the Church, and from whom He prescribed and showed that unity should originate, the Lord first gave this power, that that which he should have loosed on earth should be loosed in heaven" (Ep. 73, ad Jubaian). "Peter also, to whom the Lord committed His sheep to be fed and guarded, on whom He established and founded the Church, says that gold and silver he has none . . ." (De Habitu. Virg., p. 356). "Peter thus speaks, upon whom the Church was to be built, teaching in the name of the Church" (Ep. 69). "Peter, upon whom the Church was founded by the condescendence of God" (De Bono Patientiae).

## *Century IV.*

S. HILARY OF POITIERS—"He upbraided Peter, to whom He had just handed the Keys of the kingdom of heaven, upon whom He was to build the Church, against which the gates of hell should not in any way prevail, who, whatsoever he should bind or loose on earth, that should remain bound or loosed in heaven. . . . Peter, the first to confess the Son of God, the foundation of the Church, the door-keeper of the heavenly kingdom, and in his judgment on earth a judge of heaven" (Tract. in Ps. 131, 4). "Peter is the first to believe, and is the Prince of the Apostleship" (Comm. in Matt., c. 7). "For this will appear to be the best, and by far the most suitable thing, that to the head, that is, to the See of the Apostle Peter, the priests of the Lord refer from each one of the provinces" (Ex Epist. Sard. Conc. ad Julium. 9).

S. OPTATUS OF MILEVIS.—"If thou dost not know, learn; if thou knowest, blush. To thee ignorance cannot be ascribed; it follows, therefore, that thou knowest. To err knowingly is a sin, for the ignorant are sometimes pardoned. Thou canst not then deny but thou knowest that, in the city of Rome, the episcopal chair was first conferred on Peter, wherein might sit of all the Apostles the head, Peter, whence he was called Cephas, that in that one chair unity might be preserved by all; nor the other Apostles each contend for a distinct chair for himself, and that whosoever should set up another chair against the single chair might at once be a schismatic and a sinner. . . . Peter therefore first occupied that pre-eminent chair, which is the first of the marks [of the Church]; to him succeeded Linus, to Linus succeeded Clement," etc., etc. . . . "You who wish to claim to yourselves the holy Church, tell us the origin of your chair" (De Schism. Donat. lib. 2). "Whence is it, then, that you strive to usurp for yourselves the keys of the kingdom of heaven, you who sacrilegiously fight against the chair of Peter by your presumption and audacity? . . . Of the aforesaid marks, then, the chair is, as we have said, the first, which we have proved is ours through Peter, and this first mark brings with it the angel" (ib.).

S. AMBROSE.—" It is that same Peter to whom He said: Thou art Peter, and upon this rock I will build My Church. Therefore, where Peter is, there is the Church; where the Church is, there death is not, but life eternal" (In Ps. 40). "Peter, after having been tempted by the devil, is set over the Church. Therefore, the Lord signified what that was, that He afterwards chose him to be the pastor of the Lord's flock" (In Ps. 43). "Who else could promptly make this profession for himself? And, therefore, because he alone amongst all makes this profession, he is set before all. . . . And now he is not commanded, as at first, to feed His lambs, nor His younger sheep, as in the second instance, but His sheep, that the more perfect might govern the more perfect" (Exp. in Luc. lib. 40). " For they have not Peter's inheritance who have not Peter's chair, which, with impious discord, they rend asunder" (De Poen. t. 2, lib. 5). "Faith, therefore, is the foundation of the Church, for not of Peter's flesh, but of his faith was it said that the gates of hell shall not prevail against it; but that confession conquered hell. And this confession has banished more than one heresy; for whilst the Church, like a good ship, is often lashed by many waves, the foundation of the Church ought to have power to withstand every heresy" (De Inc. t. 2, c. 4).

S. JEROME (See page 89).—"But you say that the Church is built upon Peter, though elsewhere, the same thing is done upon all the Apostles, and all receive the keys of the kingdom of heaven; nevertheless, one is chosen out of the twelve in order that a head being appointed, the occasion of schism should be eliminated" (Adv. Jov. t. 2).

EUSEBIUS.—"The providence of the universal Ruler led as it were by the hand to Rome, Peter, that most powerful and great one of the Apostles, and, on account of his virtue, the leader of the rest, against that sad destroyer of the human race. He, like a noble general of God, armed with heavenly weapons, brought the precious merchandise of intellectual light from the East to those who dwelled in the West" (H.E. lib. 2).

S. CYRIL OF JERUSALEM.—"Peter, the chiefest and foremost of the Apostles, thrice denied the Lord in presence of a little maid, but, being moved to repentance, he wept bitterly" (Catech. 2, 15). "And all being silent (for it was beyond man to learn), Peter, the foremost of the Apostles and chief herald of the Church, not using words of his own, nor persuaded by human reasoning, but with his mind enlightened by the Father, says to Him: Thou art the Christ, nor simply that, but the Son of the living God. And a blessing follows the utterance. . . . Blessed art thou," etc. (Catech. 11, 3).

S. Ephraem.—" Have they not even respected the sentence of the Apostle, who condemns such as say, I am of Cephas? But, if the sheep were bound to refuse the name of Cephas, notwithstanding that he was the Prince of the Apostles, and had received the keys, and was accounted the shepherd of the flock, what execration is to be deemed too dreadful for him who does not dread to designate sheep that are not his by his own name?" (Serm. 56, adv. Haer.). "We hail thee, Peter, the tongue of the disciples, the voice of the heralds, the eye of the Apostles, the keeper of heaven, the first-born of those that bear the keys" (t. 3, Gr. in SS. Ap.).

S. Gregory of Nyssa.—" Peter associates himself with the Lamb, with his whole soul, and by means of the change of his name, he is changed by the Lord into something more divine; instead of Simon, being both called and having become a Rock (Peter)" (Hom. 15 in Cant. Cantic.). "Through Peter He gave to the Bishops the key of the heavenly honours" (De Castig. t. 2).

S. Gregory of Nazianzum.—"Seest thou that of the disciples of Christ, all of whom were great and worthy of the choice, one is called a Rock, and is entrusted with the foundations of the Church" (t. 1. or. 26). "Peter, who became the unbroken Rock, and to whom the Keys were delivered" (t. 2 Carm. 2).

S. EPIPHANIUS.—"And the Blessed Peter, who for awhile denied the Lord; Peter, who was the chiefest of the Apostles, he who became unto us truly a firm Rock upon which is based the Lord's faith, upon which the Church is in every way built. . . . Moreover, he then also became a firm Rock of the building, and foundation of the house of God, in that having denied Christ, and being again converted, being both found of the Lord, and found worthy to hear: Feed My sheep and feed My lambs" (Adv. Haer. 59). "He heard from that same God: Peter, feed My lambs; to him was entrusted the flock; he leads the way admirably in the power of his own Master" (In Anchor. t. 2 9).

S. JOHN CHRYSOSTOM.—See page 48.

## Century V.

S. AUGUSTINE.—"In these words of the Apostolic See—ancient and solidly built as it is—the Catholic faith is so certain and clear that it is not lawful for Christians to call it in question" (Ep. 157). See page 44.

# APPENDIX

S. Cyril of Alexandria.—See page 52.

Council of Ephesus.—In this third General Council of the Church the Pope's Legate thus addressed the two hundred Bishops there assembled: "It is doubtful to none, yea, rather, it has been known to all ages, that the holy and most Blessed Peter, the prince and head of the Apostles, the pillar of the faith, the foundation of the Catholic Church, received the keys of the kingdom from our Lord Jesus Christ, the Saviour and Redeemer of the human race, and to him was given power to bind and to loose sins; who even to the present day, and always, both lives and judges in his successors. In accordance, therefore, with this order his successor, who holds his place, our holy and most blessed Father Celestine, has sent us to this Synod to supply his presence" (Concil. Eph. Act. 3, Labbe. t. 3).